Big Book of Tissue Toppers™

Edited by Judy Crow

the Needlecraft Shop

Big Book of Tissue Toppers™

Editor Judy Crow
Art Director Brad Snow
Publishing Services Manager Brenda Gallmeyer

Managing Editor Dianne Schmidt
Assistant Art Director Nick Pierce
Copy Supervisor Michelle Beck
Copy Editors Amanda Ladig, Mary O'Donnell
Technical Editor June Sprunger

Graphic Arts Supervisor Ronda Bechinski
Book Design Nick Pierce
Graphic Artists Debby Keel, Edith Teegarden
Production Assistants Marj Morgan, Judy Neuenschwander

Photogrpahy Supervisor Tammy Christian
Photography Scott Campbell
Photography Assistant Martha Coquat

Printed in China
First Printing: 2009
Library of Congress Control Number: 2008923304
Hardcover ISBN: 978-1-57367-316-7

Every effort has been made to ensure the accuracy and completeness of the instructions in this book. However, we cannot be responsible for human error or for the results when using materials other than those specified in the instructions, or for variations in individual work.

DRGbooks.com

1 2 3 4 5 6 7 8 9

Welcome!

Of all the things I've ever stitched in plastic canvas, tissue toppers are my favorite. My first project in plastic canvas was a tissue topper. I was 10 years old. It was great for a beginning stitcher because I didn't have to have much instruction from Mom; it was pretty self-explanatory. I was so proud of my finished project.

Our designers did a fantastic job of coming up with some very unique designs. They have certainly evolved from the simple four sides and top that I started out stitching to some very innovative shapes.

In this great collection of tissue covers, you'll find something for everyone, from a country quilt look, pretty florals, fun and whimsical, to sports, animals and beautiful holiday designs.

Happy Stitching!

Judy Crow

Contents

Long Stitch

Quilt Look

Potpourri

Holiday

Christmas Cottage

Design by Angie Arickx

Skill Level

Intermediate

Size

Fits boutique-style tissue box

Materials

- 3 sheets 7-count plastic canvas
- Red Heart Super Saver Art. E300 medium weight yarn as listed in color key
- Red Heart Classic Art. E267 medium weight yarn as listed in color key
- #16 tapestry needle
- Hot-glue gun

Cutting & Stitching

1. Cut plastic canvas according to graphs (pages 9, 10, 11 and 38).

2. Stitch pieces following graphs, filling in around doors and windows on front, back and sides with hot red stitch pattern. Leave area indicated on fence tray base unstitched.

3. When background stitching is completed, work Backstitches on

chimney sides and French Knots on front door and fence evergreen swags.

Assembly

1. For fence, Overcast inside edges and top edges of long and short sides. With wrong sides facing, Whipstitch long sides to short sides. With right side of base facing up, Whipstitch base to sides.

2. Whipstitch cottage front, back and sides together; Overcast top and bottom edges.

3. Whipstitch chimney sides together; Overcast top and bottom edges.

4. Using white, Overcast corner edges and back edges of roof pieces A and B, going through each hole only once. With right sides facing, Whipstitch corner edges of A and B pieces together, going through corner holes only and making four pairs of joined corners.

5. Whipstitch pairs together at peak edges with paddy green. Using white, Whipstitch eaves from blue dot to blue dot to front edges; Overcast remaining unworked edges.

6. Insert chimney into roof opening and secure with glue. Place roof on cottage; glue eaves to top edges of cottage.

7. Insert tissue box and place cottage in fence tray over unstitched area of base. ∎

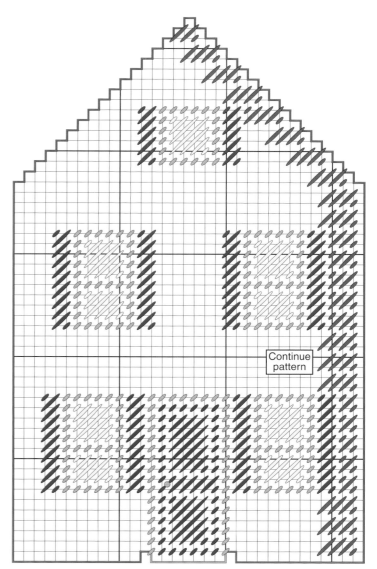

Continue pattern

Cottage Front
33 holes x 53 holes
Cut 1

COLOR KEY	
Yards	**Medium Weight Yarn**
64 (58.5m)	☐ White #311
8 (7.4m)	▨ Gold #321
6 (5.5m)	☐ Pale yellow #322
22 (20.2m)	■ Paddy green #368
6 (5.5m)	■ Burgundy #376
70 (64m)	■ Hot red #390
40 (36.6m)	▨ Emerald green #676
	╱ White #311 Backstitch
	● Gold #321 French Knot
	● Hot red #390 French Knot

Color numbers given are for Red Heart Super Saver Art. E300 and Classic Art. E267 medium weight yarn.

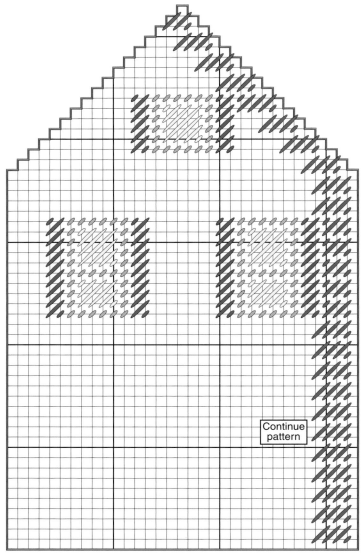

Cottage Side & Back
33 holes x 53 holes
Cut 3

Continue pattern

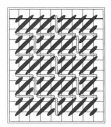

Chimney Side
9 holes x 11 holes
Cut 4

COLOR KEY

Yards	Medium Weight Yarn
64 (58.5m)	☐ White #311
8 (7.4m)	▨ Gold #321
6 (5.5m)	☐ Pale yellow #322
22 (20.2m)	■ Paddy green #368
6 (5.5m)	■ Burgundy #376
70 (64m)	■ Hot red #390
40 (36.6m)	▨ Emerald green #676
	╱ White #311 Backstitch
	● Gold #321 French Knot
	● Hot red #390 French Knot

Color numbers given are for Red Heart Super Saver Art. E300 and Classic Art. E267 medium weight yarn.

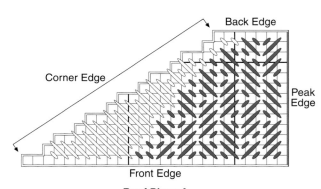

Back Edge

Corner Edge

Peak Edge

Front Edge

Roof Piece A
25 holes x 13 holes
Cut 4

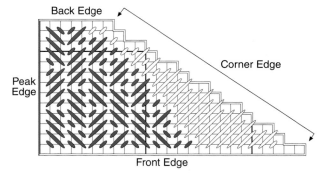

Back Edge

Peak Edge

Corner Edge

Front Edge

Roof Piece B
25 holes x 13 holes
Cut 4

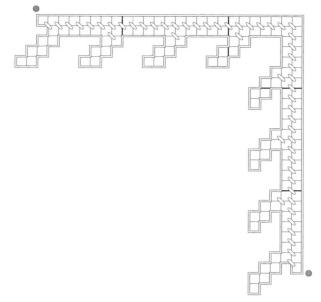

Roof Eaves
27 holes x 27 holes
Cut 4

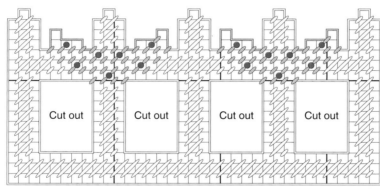

Fence Tray Short Side
35 holes x 17 holes
Cut 2

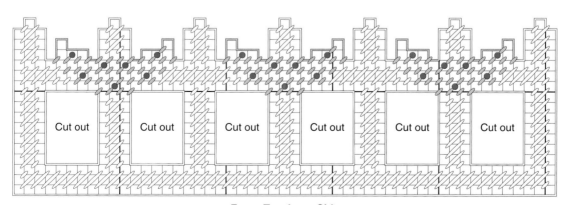

Fence Tray Long Side
51 holes x 17 holes
Cut 2

Graphs continued on page 38

Santa

Design by Laura Victory

Skill Level

Intermediate

Size

Fits boutique-style tissue box

Materials

- 4 sheets 7-count plastic canvas
- Uniek Needloft plastic canvas yarn as listed in color key
- Soft chenillelike *or* chenillelike eyelash bulky weight yarn as listed in color key
- #16 tapestry needle
- 4 (8mm) round black beads
- 2 (15mm) red sparkle pompom
- 6 (1¼-inch/30mm) red Christmas bows
- 1 sheet each red and green felt
- Powdered blush
- Hand-sewing needle
- Black sewing thread
- Hot-glue gun

Instructions

1. Cut plastic canvas according to graphs (pages 14, 15 and 39). Cut two 30-hole x 8-hole pieces for coaster holder bases.

2. Cut two pieces each red and green felt slightly smaller than coasters. Cut four pieces green felt slightly smaller than holder sides. Cut two pieces red felt slightly smaller than top portion of hats above cuffs.

3. Stitch coaster holder bases with holly Continental Stitches.

4. Following graphs throughout all stitching, stitch and Overcast hats, hat pompoms and mustaches. Stitch and Overcast two coasters, working uncoded areas with eggshell Continental Stitches. Stitch and Overcast remaining two coasters replacing holly with red.

5. Stitch remaining pieces, working uncoded areas with eggshell Continental Stitches and reversing two holder sides before stitching.

Assembly

1. For eyes, use hand-sewing needle and black thread to attach black beads to faces where indicated.

2. Glue felt to backs of hats and holder sides, trimming felt on sides as needed to keep edges free for Overcasting and Whipstitching.

3. For each coaster holder, using eggshell throughout, Whipstitch one front to two sides between green dots, then Whipstitch front and sides to one base. Overcast top edges of front and sides.

4. For tissue cover, Overcast inside edges on top; Overcast bottom edges of faces.

5. Place coaster holders next to tissue cover sides. Using eggshell through step 6, Whipstitch faces to cover sides, attaching holder sides between brackets while Whipstitching.

6. Whipstitch back edges of holder bases to bottom edges of cover sides. Whipstitch cover faces and sides to top.

Finishing

1. Glue red felt to backs of red coasters and green felt to backs of green coasters.

2. Glue one bow to each coaster and to coaster holder front pieces where indicated on graphs.

3. Glue hats to faces between blue dots.

4. Glue mustaches to faces where indicated with blue lines. Glue hat pompoms on tips of hats.

5. For noses, glue red glitter pompoms to faces between eyes and mustaches where indicated. ∎

COLOR KEY	
Yards	**Plastic Canvas Yarn**
76 (69.5m)	■ Red #01
69 (63.1m)	■ Holly #27
21 (19.3m)	☐ Pale peach #56
54 (53.1m)	Uncoded areas are eggshell #39 Continental Stitches
	⁄ Eggshell #39 Overcast and Whipstitch
	Bulky Weight Yarn
18 (16.5m)	☐ Cream
	● Attach black bead
	● Attach red pompom
	✸ Attach red bow
Color numbers given are for Uniek Needloft plastic canvas yarn.	

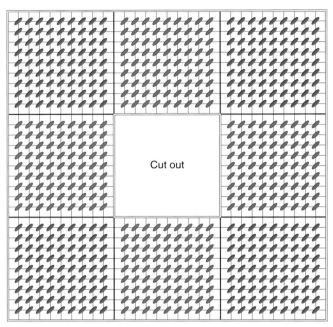

Cover Top
30 holes x 30 holes
Cut 1

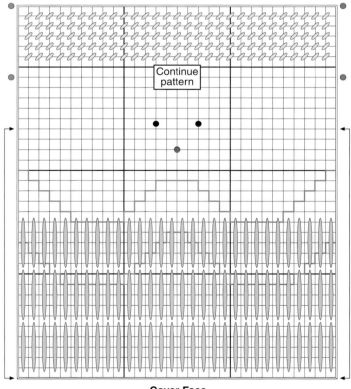

Cover Face
30 holes x 36 holes
Cut 2

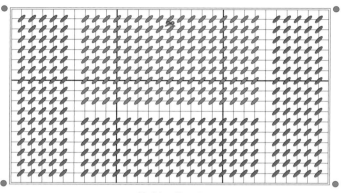

Holder Front
30 holes x 17 holes
Cut 2

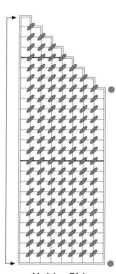

Holder Side
8 holes x 24 holes
Cut 4, reverse 2

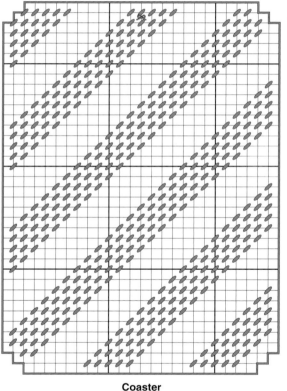

Coaster
26 holes x 36 holes
Cut 4
Stitch 2 as graphed
Stitch 2 replacing
holly with red

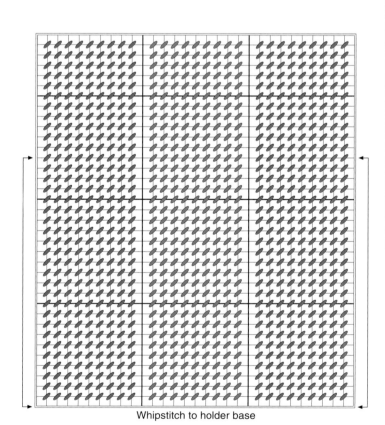

Whipstitch to holder base

Cover Side
30 holes x 36 holes
Cut 2

Graphs continued on page 39

Snowman

Design by Nancy Dorman

Skill Level

Beginner

Size

Fits boutique-style tissue box

Materials

- 2 sheets 7-count plastic canvas
- Medium weight yarn as listed in color key
- #16 tapestry needle

Project Note

Depending on size of boutique-style tissue box, this topper may be a very tight fit.

Instructions

1. Cut plastic canvas according to graphs (pages 17 and 18).

2. Stitch topper pieces following graphs.

3. Using Christmas green throughout, Overcast inside edges on top and bottom edges of sides. Using a Binding Stitch (page 18) or Whipstitch, stitch sides together, then stitch sides to top.

4. Stitch and Overcast snowman following graph, working uncoded areas with white Continental Stitches.

5. When background stitching is completed, work black and orange French Knots where indicated.

6. Center and tack snowman to one side with white yarn, making sure bottom edges of snowman's foot and side are even. ■

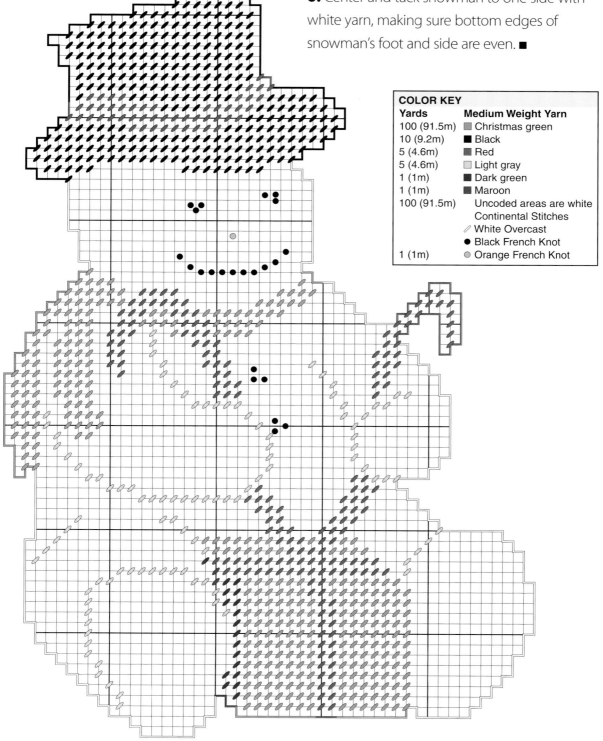

COLOR KEY		
Yards		**Medium Weight Yarn**
100 (91.5m)	▨	Christmas green
10 (9.2m)	■	Black
5 (4.6m)	▨	Red
5 (4.6m)	▢	Light gray
1 (1m)	▨	Dark green
1 (1m)	■	Maroon
100 (91.5m)		Uncoded areas are white Continental Stitches
	╱	White Overcast
	●	Black French Knot
1 (1m)	●	Orange French Knot

Snowman
50 holes x 72 holes
Cut 1

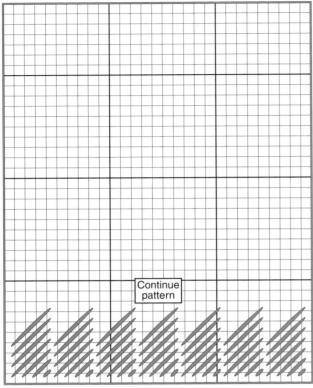

Side
29 holes x 37 holes
Cut 4

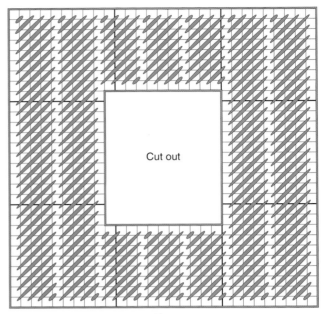

Top
29 holes x 29 holes
Cut 1

COLOR KEY	
Yards	**Medium Weight Yarn**
100 (91.5m)	▨ Christmas green
10 (9.2m)	■ Black
5 (4.6m)	■ Red
5 (4.6m)	□ Light gray
1 (1m)	■ Dark green
1 (1m)	■ Maroon
100 (91.5m)	Uncoded areas are white Continental Stitches
	╱ White Overcast
	● Black French Knot
1 (1m)	● Orange French Knot

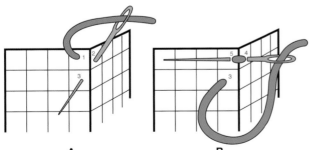

A
Work first stitch as
shown from 1 to 2
Wrap yarn around
back of canvas,
bringing needle up at 3

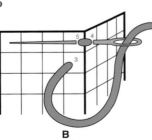

B
Wrap yarn around front
of canvas, bringing needle
down at 4 and up at 5

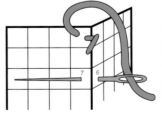

C
Bring needle around
front of canvas, down at 6,
and back up at 7

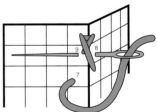

D
Continue working
stitch pattern,
covering all edges

Binding Stitch

Poinsettia

Design by Nancy Dorman

Skill Level

Intermediate

Size

Fits boutique-style tissue box

Materials

- 2 sheets 10-count plastic canvas
- Light weight yarn as listed in color key
- 2mm cloisonné thread as listed in color key
- #18 tapestry needle
- 36 (3mm) gold metallic beads
- Beading needle
- Green and white sewing thread

Instructions

1. Cut plastic canvas according to graphs (pages 20 and 21).

2. Stitch poinsettias following graph, working Continental Stitches in uncoded areas as follows: white background with red, green background with green. Overcast with red and green.

3. Stitch topper pieces following graphs, working green Backstitches when background stitching is completed.

4. Using beading needle throughout, attach gold beads to topper pieces with white thread, and to poinsettias with green thread where indicated on graphs.

5. Center and tack poinsettias to sides with red yarn.

6. Using red throughout, Overcast inside edges on top and bottom edges of sides. Using a Binding Stitch (page 18) or Whipstitch, stitch sides together, then stitch sides to top. ■

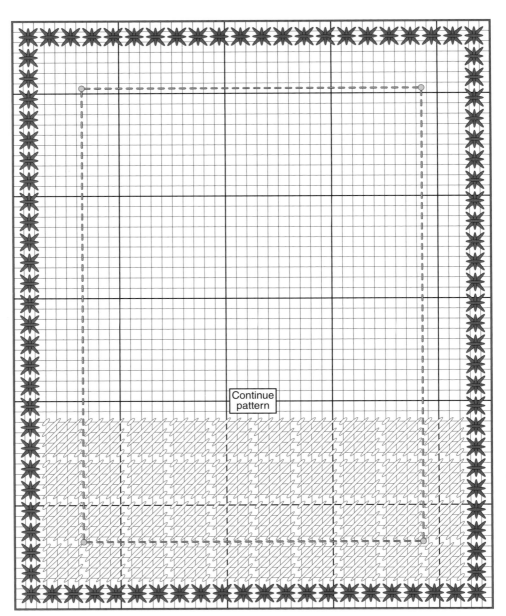

Side
45 holes x 57 holes
Cut 4

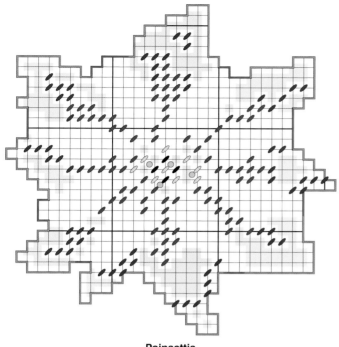

COLOR KEY

Yards	Light Weight Yarn
150 (137.2m)	☐ White
100 (91.5m)	■ Red
5 (4.6m)	■ Maroon
5 (4.6m)	■ Dark green
3 (2.8m)	■ Black
	Uncoded areas on white background are red Continental Stitches
50 (45.7m)	Uncoded areas on green background are green Continental Stitches
	⁄ Green Backstitch and Overcast
	Cloisonné Thread
3 (2.8m)	☐ Gold
	● Attach gold bead

Poinsettia
31 holes x 32 holes
Cut 4

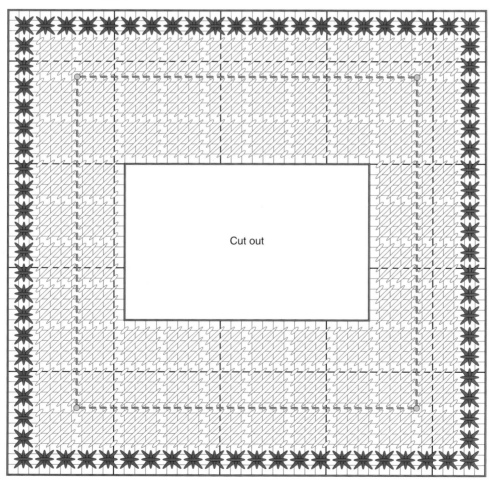

Cut out

Top
45 holes x 45 holes
Cut 1

Hearts Delight

Design by Janelle Giese

Skill Level

Advanced

Size

Fits boutique-style tissue box

Materials

- 1½ sheets 7-count plastic canvas
- Red Heart Classic Art. E267 medium weight yarn as listed in color key
- Red Heart Super Saver Art. E300 medium weight yarn as listed in color key
- Red Heart Kids Art. E711 medium weight yarn as listed in color key
- Kreinik Heavy (#32) Braid as listed in color key
- DMC #3 pearl cotton as listed in color key
- #16 tapestry needle

Cutting & Stitching

1. Cut plastic canvas according to graphs (pages 40 and 41).

2. Stitch pieces following graphs, working uncoded areas with dark orchid Continental Stitches and working Straight Stitches where indicated for some of the background stitching.

Front Embroidery

1. Using full strands yarn throughout, work accents as follows: pink for eyelids, black for back arm and white for sole of shoe. Use grenadine to Straight Stitch hearts on bottom border.

2. Using pearl cotton throughout, work Lazy Daisy Stitches for flower petals. Straight Stitch center of bottom medium electric blue flower with tangerine. Work black embroidery next, wrapping French Knot of exclamation point two times. Work white embroidery, wrapping French Knots one time.

3. Use crimson braid to work Backstitches where indicated to complete embroidery on front.

Back, Sides & Top Embroidery

1. Begin by using a full strand of grenadine to stitch hearts on bottom border.

2. Complete bottom border by first working black pearl cotton embroidery, then white.

3. For remaining areas, stitch embroidery in following order: purple braid, black pearl cotton, crimson braid.

Continued on page 40

Hearts

Design by Deborah Scheblein

Skill Level
Beginner

Size
Fits boutique-style tissue box

Materials
- 1½ sheets 7-count plastic canvas
- Medium weight yarn as listed in color key
- 6-strand embroidery floss as listed in color key
- #16 tapestry needle

Instructions
1. Cut plastic canvas according to graphs.

2. Stitch pieces following graphs, working uncoded areas with white Continental Stitches.

3. When background stitching is completed, work burgundy Backstitches around hearts.

4. Overcast inside edges on top with bright pink. Using white Whipstitch sides A to sides, then Whipstitch sides to top; Overcast bottom edges. ■

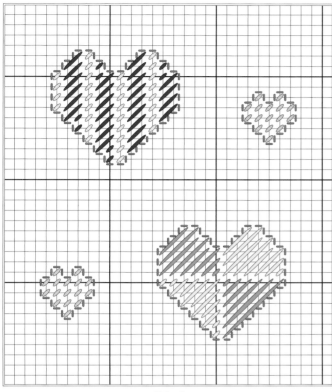

Side A
31 holes x 37 holes
Cut 2

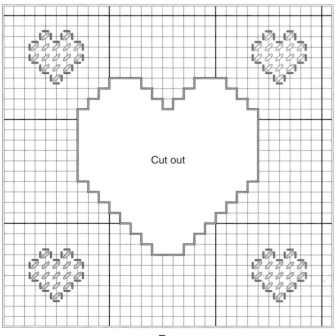

Top
31 holes x 31 holes
Cut 1

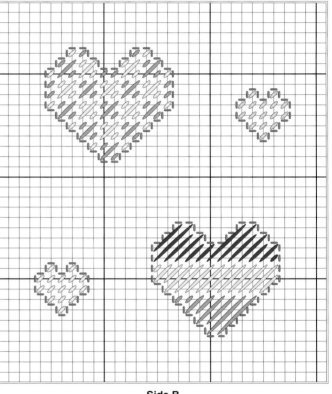

Side B
31 holes x 37 holes
Cut 2

COLOR KEY	
Yards	**Medium Weight Yarn**
5 (4.6m)	▨ Bright pink
4 (3.7m)	☐ Yellow
3 (2.8m)	■ Burgundy
3 (2.8m)	☐ Lavender
1 (1m)	☐ Light pink
1 (1m)	☐ Light green
1 (1m)	☐ Light orange
67 (61.3m)	Uncoded areas are white Continental Stitches
	⁄ White Overcast and Whipstitch
	6-Strand Embroidery Floss
11 (10.1m)	⁄ Burgundy Backstitch

Red, White & Blue

Design by D.K. Designs

Skill Level

Intermediate

Size

Fits boutique-style tissue box

Materials

- 2½ sheets 7-count plastic canvas
- 5 (5-inch) Uniek QuickShape plastic canvas stars
- Red Heart Super Saver Art. E300 medium weight yarn as listed in color key
- #16 tapestry needle
- 4 (½-inch/11.4cm) white star-shaped buttons
- Hot-glue gun

Instructions

1. Cut plastic canvas according to graphs (pages 27 and 42), cutting away gray areas on stars.

2. Stitch pieces following graphs. Overcast stars, background sides and top, and inside edges of side and top frames.

3. Using photo as a guide through

step 6, glue white star buttons to center of each side star.

4. Center and glue frames over corresponding background pieces, leaving edges free for stitching.

5. Center and glue side stars to background sides. Center and glue top star over opening on background top.

6. Whipstitch side frames together, then Whipstitch side frames to top frame. Overcast bottom edges. ■

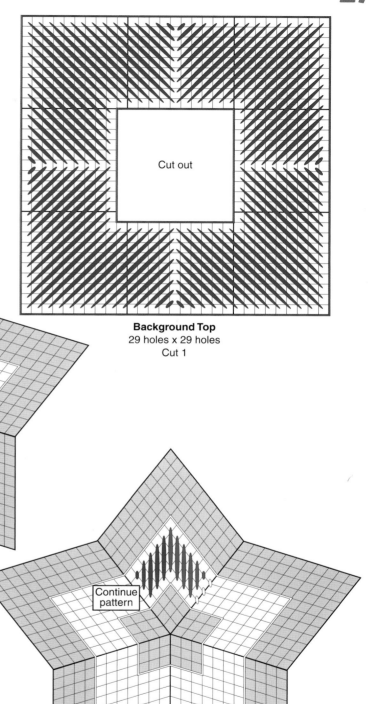

Background Top
29 holes x 29 holes
Cut 1

Cut out

Continue pattern

Side Star
Cut 4 from plastic canvas stars,
cutting away gray area

Continue pattern

Top Star
Cut 1 from plastic canvas star,
cutting away gray areas

COLOR KEY

Yards	Medium Weight Yarn
20 (18.3m)	☐ White #311
72 (65.9m)	■ Burgundy #376
25 (22.9m)	■ Soft navy #387
	☆ Attach star button

Color numbers given are for Red Heart Super Saver Art. E300 medium weight yarn.

Graphs continued on page 42

Star-Spangled

Design by Angie Arickx

Skill Level

Intermediate

Size

Fits family-size tissue box

Materials

- 1½ sheets 7-count plastic canvas
- Red Heart Super Saver Art. E300 medium weight yarn as listed in color key
- #16 tapestry needle

Instructions

1. Cut plastic canvas according to graphs. (pages 29 and 43).

2. Stitch pieces following graphs.

3. Overcast inside edges on top and bottom edges of sides and ends. Whipstitch sides to ends, then Whipstitch sides and ends to top. ∎

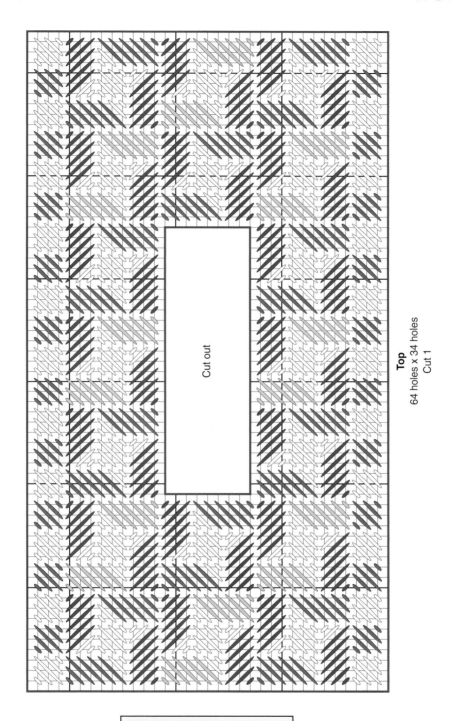

Top
64 holes x 34 holes
Cut 1

Cut out

COLOR KEY

Yards	Medium Weight Yarn
32 (29.3m)	☐ White #311
29 (26.6m)	◼ Burgundy #376
28 (25.7m)	◼ Soft navy #387
40 (36.6m)	◼ Hot red #390
28 (25.7m)	◻ Blue #886

Color numbers given are for Red Heart
Super Saver Art. E300 medium weight
yarn.

Graphs continued on page 43

Game Time

Design by Betty Hansen

Skill Level

Intermediate

Size

Fits boutique-style tissue box

Materials

- 4 sheets stiff 7-count plastic canvas
- Medium weight yarn as listed in color key
- #16 tapestry needle
- ½-inch (1.3cm) white plastic ring
- 10 golf tees: 5 each in two colors (sample used blue and white)

Cutting & Stitching

1. Cut plastic canvas according to graphs (pages 32, 33 and 34), cutting out opening in front lining only, leaving back lining intact. Cut three 37-hole x 29-hole pieces for side linings and drawer support. Drawer front and all lining pieces will remain unstitched.

2. Stitch drawer face, base, sides and back following graphs. Stitch topper sides, back, front and top following graphs.

3. Using white throughout, Overcast opening on topper front piece. Place unstitched topper top lining under stitched top, matching edges.

Whipstitch inside edges together through both layers.

Topper Assembly

1. Using navy blue, Whipstitch front and back linings to side linings. Whipstitch top edges of front, back and sides to drawer support. Set aside.

2. For topper pieces, using navy blue through step 4, Whipstitch sides to back, then Whipstitch sides and back to top, working through all layers when attaching top.

3. Whipstitch topper front to sides, beginning at bottom and working up. *Note: Front piece is shorter than sides so there will be eight holes left at top of each side for drawer.* Overcast all remaining edges at top front of topper.

4. Insert lining in topper, then Whipstitch bottom edges of lining and topper together.

Drawer Assembly

1. Using navy blue and with right sides facing, Whipstitch sides to back and unstitched front. Whipstitch front, back and sides to base. Overcast top edges of sides and back, leaving top edge of front unworked at this time.

2. Center drawer face over drawer front, then Whipstitch top edges together with

navy. Overcast remaining edges
following graph.

3. For drawer pull, use navy yarn to
attach top of plastic ring to drawer face,
where indicated, working through
both layers.

4. Insert drawer in slot on topper.
Store golf tees in drawer to use as game
pieces for tic-tac-toe. ■

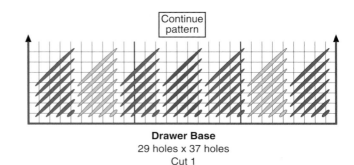

Drawer Base
29 holes x 37 holes
Cut 1

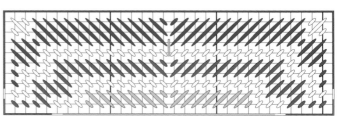

Drawer Face
31 holes x 10 holes
Cut 1

Topper Back
31 holes x 39 holes
Cut 1

Whipstitch to drawer support

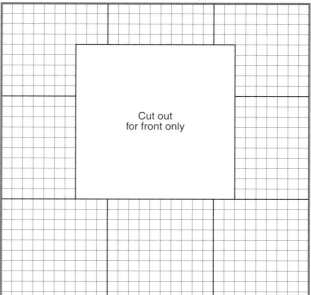

Topper Front & Back Lining
29 holes x 29 holes
Cut 2
Do not stitch

COLOR KEY

Yards	Medium Weight Yarn
63 (57.7m)	■ Navy blue
35 (32m)	□ White
29 (26.6m)	■ Red
28 (25.7m)	□ Royal blue
	▯ Attach plastic ring

Cut out
for front only

Topper Side
39 holes x 39 holes
Cut 2

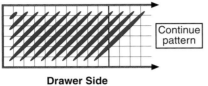

Drawer Side
37 holes x 6 holes
Cut 2

Drawer Front & Back
29 holes x 6 holes
Cut 2
Do not stitch front

Front Edge

Topper Top & Top Lining
31 holes x 39 holes
Cut 2, stitch 1

Top Edge

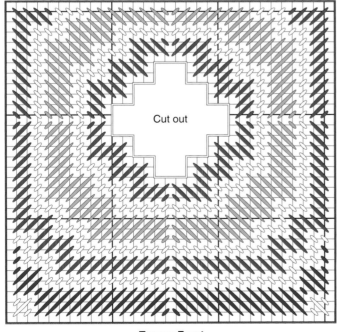

Cut out

Topper Front
31 holes x 31 holes
Cut 1

COLOR KEY	
Yards	**Medium Weight Yarn**
63 (57.7m)	■ Navy blue
35 (32m)	□ White
29 (26.6m)	■ Red
28 (25.7m)	▨ Royal blue
	∣ Attach plastic ring

Halloween

Design by Mildred Goeppel

Skill Level

Intermediate

Size

Fits boutique-style tissue box

Materials

- 1½ sheets black 7-count plastic canvas
- Medium weight yarn as listed in color key
- Plastic canvas yarn as listed in color key
- 6-strand embroidery floss as listed in color key
- #16 tapestry needle
- 2 (1-inch/25mm) cat eyes
- 12 (10mm) movable eyes
- 2 (3mm) movable eyes
- Button shank remover or wire cutters
- Hot-glue gun

Instructions

1. Cut plastic canvas according to graphs (pages 36 and 37). ***Note:*** *Pumpkin and witch sides are two holes narrower than cat and ghost sides.*

2. Stitch pieces following graphs, working Continental Stitches in uncoded areas as follows: white background with dark blue, gray background with black medium weight yarn, peach background with bright orange. Bar indicated with blue line on pumpkin side will remain unstitched.

3. Stitch uncoded areas on yellow background with yellow Reverse Continental Stitches.

4. When background stitching is completed, work dark gray Backstitches and Straight Stitches on cat and orange Backstitches on pumpkin.

5. Using floss throughout, work lilac Backstitches to outline cat, and black Backstitches and Straight Stitches for tree branches on witch side and for lettering on tombstone on ghost side. Work black French Knot for ghost's mouth.

6. Using bright orange throughout, Overcast inside edges on top and bottom edges of sides. Whipstitch pumpkin and witch sides to cat and ghost sides, making sure to place pumpkin and witch sides opposite each other, and cat and ghost sides opposite each other. Whipstitch sides to top.

7. Using button shank remover or wire cutters, cut shanks from cat eyes; glue to cat where indicated. Glue 3mm eyes to ghost where indicated. Glue 6mm eyes to pumpkin side and top where indicated. ■

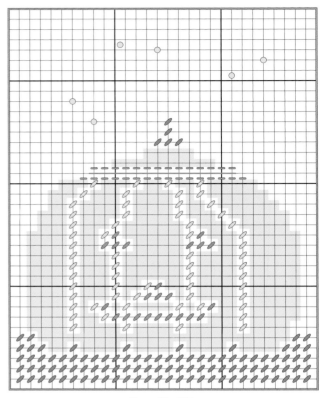

Pumpkin Side
29 holes x 37 holes
Cut 1

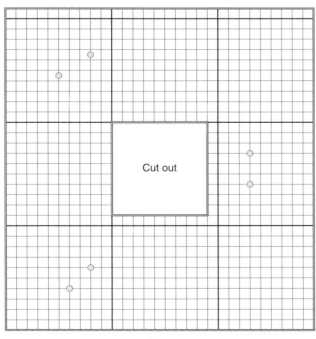

Top
29 holes x 31 holes
Cut 1

Cut out

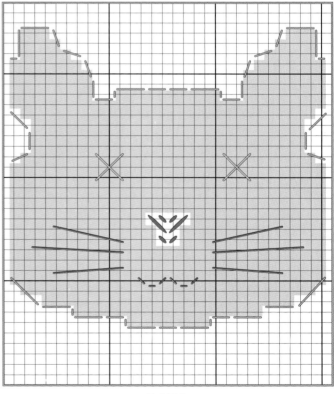

Cat Side
31 holes x 37 holes
Cut 1

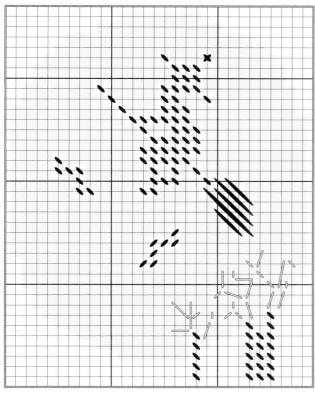

Witch Side
29 holes x 37 holes
Cut 1

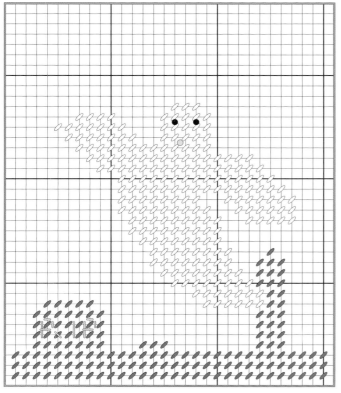

Ghost Side
31 holes x 37 holes
Cut 1

COLOR KEY	
Yards	**Medium Weight Yarn**
12 (11m)	Black
4 (3.7m)	White
3 (2.8m)	Dark gray
3 (2.8m)	Green
2 (1.9m)	Light orange
37 (33.9m)	Uncoded areas on white background are dark blue Continental Stitches
16 (14.7m)	Uncoded areas on gray background are black Continental Stitches
14 (12.9m)	Uncoded areas on peach background are bright orange Continental Stitches
10 (9.2m)	Uncoded areas on yellow background are yellow Reverse Continental Stitches
	Bright orange Backstitch, Overcast and Whipstitch
	Dark gray Backstitch and Straight Stitch
	Plastic Canvas Yarn
3 (2.8m)	Black
	6-Strand Embroidery Floss
2 (1.9m)	Black Backstitch and Straight Stitch
2 (1.9m)	Lilac Backstitch
	Black French Knot
	Attach cat eye
	Attach 10mm movable eye
	Attach 3mm movable eye

Christmas Cottage

Continued from page 11

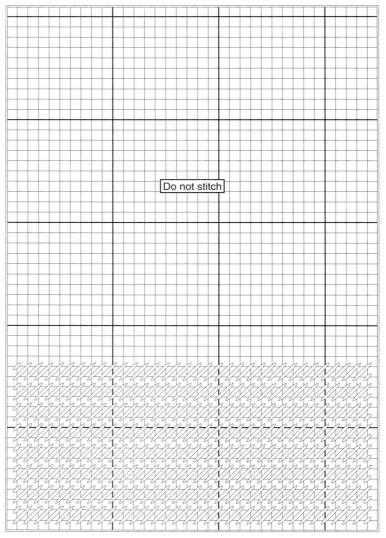

Do not stitch

Fence Tray Base
35 holes x 51 holes
Cut 1

COLOR KEY	
Yards	**Medium Weight Yarn**
64 (58.5m)	☐ White #311
8 (7.4m)	▨ Gold #321
6 (5.5m)	☐ Pale yellow #322
22 (20.2m)	■ Paddy green #368
6 (5.5m)	■ Burgundy #376
70 (64m)	■ Hot red #390
40 (36.6m)	▨ Emerald green #676
	╱ White #311 Backstitch
	◉ Gold #321 French Knot
	● Hot red #390 French Knot

Color numbers given are for Red Heart Super Saver Art. E300 and Classic Art. E267 medium weight yarn.

Continued from page 15

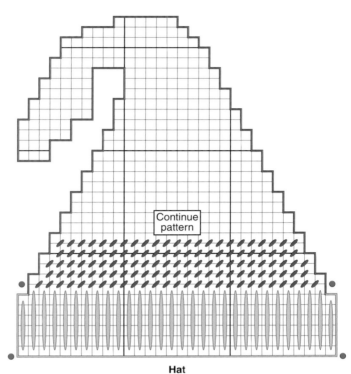

Pompom
6 holes x 6 holes
Cut 2

Continue
pattern

Hat
30 holes x 33 holes
Cut 2

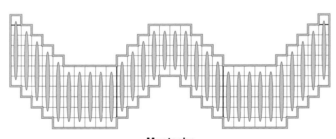

Mustache
30 holes x 11 holes
Cut 2

COLOR KEY	
Yards	**Plastic Canvas Yarn**
76 (69.5m)	■ Red #01
69 (63.1m)	■ Holly #27
21 (19.3m)	□ Pale peach #56
54 (53.1m)	Uncoded areas are eggshell #39 Continental Stitches
	⁄ Eggshell #39 Overcast and Whipstitch
	Bulky Weight Yarn
18 (16.5m)	▨ Cream
	● Attach black bead
	● Attach red pompom
	✺ Attach red bow

Color numbers given are for Uniek Needloft plastic canvas yarn.

Continued from page 22

Assembly

1. Using black yarn, Overcast inside edges of top and bottom edges of sides.

2. Using black and dark orchid, Whipstitch front and back to sides. Whipstitch front, back and sides to top with black. ∎

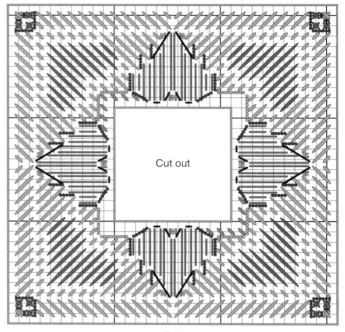

Top
31 holes x 31 holes
Cut 1

Front
31 holes x 37 holes
Cut 1

COLOR KEY

Yards	Medium Weight Yarn
2 (1.9m)	☐ White #1
30 (27.5m)	■ Black #12
1 (1m)	☐ Eggshell #111
19 (17.4m)	▨ Grenadine #730
14 (12.9m)	■ Dark orchid #776
25 (22.9m)	■ Country red #914
1 (1m)	■ Cardinal #917

Uncoded areas are dark orchid #776 Continental Stitches

⁄ White #1 Straight Stitch
⁄ Black #12 Straight Stitch
1 (1m) ⁄ Emerald green #676 Straight Stitch
⁄ Grenadine #730 Straight Stitch
1 (1m) ⁄ Pink #737 Straight Stitch
⁄ Dark orchid #776 Straight Stitch
1 (1m) ⁄ Lime #2652 (4-ply) Straight Stitch
⁄ Lime #2652 (2-ply) Backstitch

Heavy (#32) Braid
4 (3.7m) ⁄ Purple Hi Lustre #012HL Straight Stitch
11 (10.1m) ⁄ Crimson #031 Backstitch and Straight Stitch

#3 Pearl Cotton
1 (1m) ⊠ Bright orange #608 (2-strand) Cross Stitch
1 (1m) ⊠ Tangerine #740 (2-strand) Cross Stitch
2 (1.9m) ⊠ Medium electric blue #996 (2-strand) Cross Stitch
5 (4.6m) ⁄ White Backstitch and Straight Stitch
12 (11m) ⁄ Black #310 Backstitch and Straight Stitch
⁄ Bright orange #608 Straight Stitch
⁄ Tangerine #740 Straight Stitch
⚬ White Lazy Daisy Stitch
⚬ Bright orange #608 Lazy Daisy Stitch
⚬ Tangerine #740 Lazy Daisy Stitch
⚬ Medium electric blue #996 Lazy Daisy Stitch
● White (1-wrap) French Knot
● Black #310 (2-wrap) French Knot

Color numbers given are for Red Heart Classic Art. E267, Super Saver Art. E300 and Kids Art. E711 medium weight yarn; Kreinik Heavy (#32) Braid and DMC #3 pearl cotton.

Back & Side
31 holes x 37 holes
Cut 3

Continued from page 27

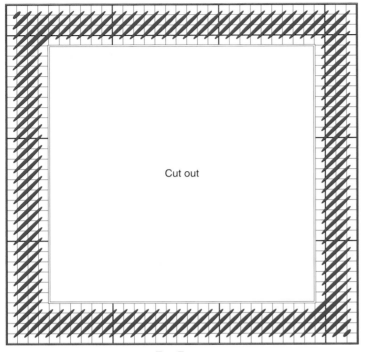

COLOR KEY

Yards	Medium Weight Yarn
20 (18.3m)	☐ White #311
72 (65.9m)	■ Burgundy #376
25 (22.9m)	■ Soft navy #387
	☆ Attach star button

Color numbers given are for Red Heart Super Saver Art. E300 medium weight yarn.

Top Frame
33 holes x 33 holes
Cut 1

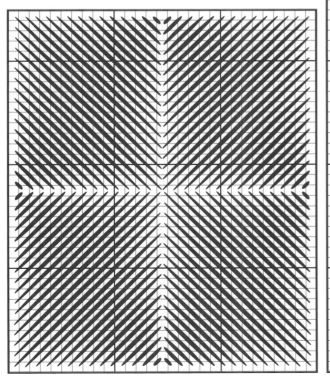

Background Side
29 holes x 35 holes
Cut 4

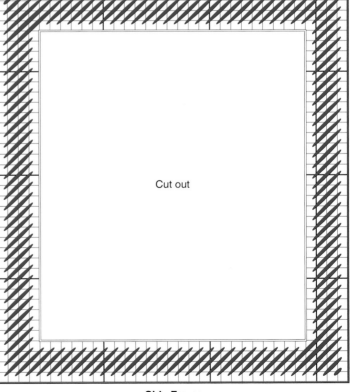

Side Frame
33 holes x 38 holes
Cut 4

Star-Spangled

Continued from page 29

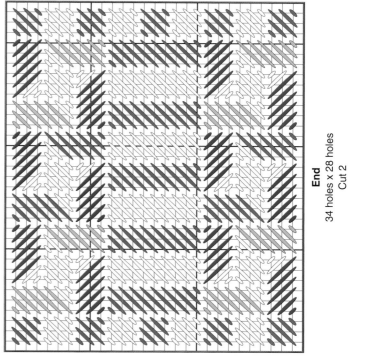

End
34 holes x 28 holes
Cut 2

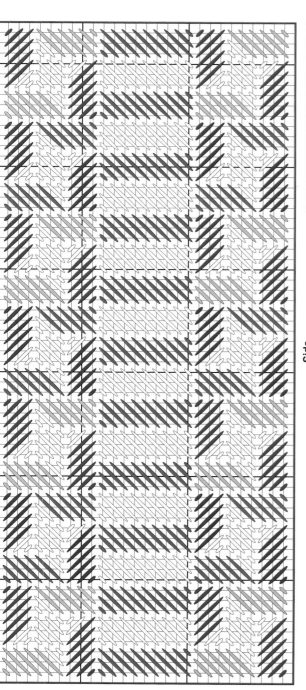

Side
64 holes x 28 holes
Cut 2

COLOR KEY	
Yards	**Medium Weight Yarn**
32 (29.3m)	☐ White #311
29 (26.6m)	■ Burgundy #376
28 (25.7m)	■ Soft navy #387
40 (36.6m)	■ Hot red #390
28 (25.7m)	▨ Blue #886

Color numbers given are for Red Heart Super Saver Art. E300 medium weight yarn.

Animals

Butterflies & Bugs

Design by Patricia Klesh

Skill Level

Intermediate

Size

Fits boutique-style tissue box

Materials

- 2 sheets clear 7-count plastic canvas
- Medium weight yarn as listed in color key
- 6-strand embroidery floss as listed in color key
- #16 tapestry needle

Project Note

Depending on size of boutique-style tissue box, this topper may be a very tight fit.

Instructions

1. Cut plastic canvas according to graphs (pages 47 and 48).

2. Stitch pieces following graphs, working yarn Backstitches and Straight Stitches as part of the background stitching and working uncoded backgrounds with light blue Continental Stitches.

3. When background stitching is completed, work yarn French Knots and embroidery floss Backstitches and Straight Stitches.

4. Using light blue, Whipstitch sides together; Whipstitch sides to top. Overcast all remaining edges. ■

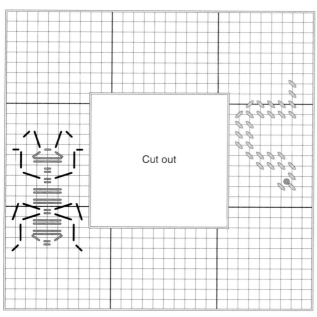

Top
29 holes x 29 holes
Cut 1

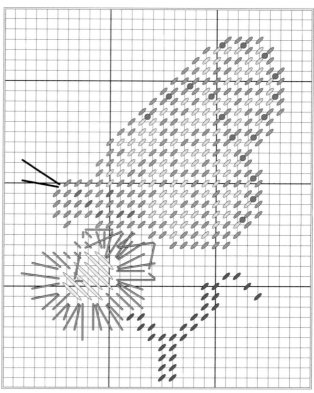

Monarch Butterfly Side
29 holes x 37 holes
Cut 1

COLOR KEY	
Yards	**Medium Weight Yarn**
7 (6.5m)	▨ Black
6 (5.5m)	▨ Olive green
5 (4.6m)	☐ Orange
3 (2.8m)	☐ Yellow
3 (2.8m)	■ Green
3 (2.8m)	☐ Off-white
2 (1.9m)	▨ Gray
2 (1.9m)	■ Brown
2 (1.9m)	■ Red
2 (1.9m)	■ White
1 (1m)	▨ Bright green
72 (65.9m)	Uncoded areas are light blue Continental Stitches
	⟋ Light blue Overcast and Whipstitch
	⟋ Black Backstitch and Straight Stitch
	⟋ Olive green Straight Stitch
	⟋ Orange Straight Stitch
	⟋ Yellow Straight Stitch
2 (1.9m)	⟋ Deep rose Straight Stitch
2 (1.9m)	⟋ Light clay Straight Stitch
	● Black French Knot
	● White French Knot
	6-Strand Embroidery Floss
4 (3.7m)	⟋ Black Backstitch and Straight Stitch
4 (3.7m)	⟋ Yellow Backstitch and Straight Stitch
2 (1.9m)	⟋ Orange Backstitch and Straight Stitch
	● Yellow French Knot

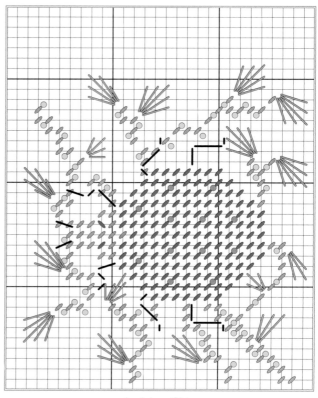

Ladybug Side
29 holes x 37 holes
Cut 1

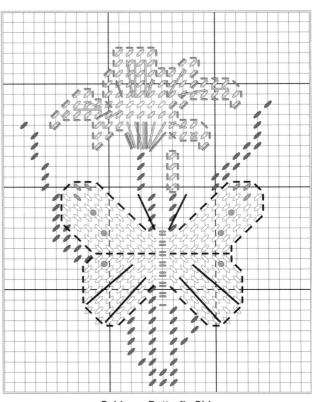

Cabbage Butterfly Side
29 holes x 37 holes
Cut 1

COLOR KEY

Yards	Medium Weight Yarn
7 (6.5m)	■ Black
6 (5.5m)	■ Olive green
5 (4.6m)	□ Orange
3 (2.8m)	□ Yellow
3 (2.8m)	■ Green
3 (2.8m)	□ Off-white
2 (1.9m)	■ Gray
2 (1.9m)	■ Brown
2 (1.9m)	■ Red
2 (1.9m)	■ White
1 (1m)	□ Bright green
72 (65.9m)	Uncoded areas are light blue Continental Stitches
	⁄ Light blue Overcast and Whipstitch
	⁄ Black Backstitch and Straight Stitch
	⁄ Olive green Straight Stitch
	⁄ Orange Straight Stitch
	⁄ Yellow Straight Stitch
2 (1.9m)	⁄ Deep rose Straight Stitch
2 (1.9m)	⁄ Light clay Straight Stitch
	● Black French Knot
	● White French Knot
	6-Strand Embroidery Floss
4 (3.7m)	⁄ Black Backstitch and Straight Stitch
4 (3.7m)	⁄ Yellow Backstitch and Straight Stitch
2 (1.9m)	⁄ Orange Backstitch and Straight Stitch
	○ Yellow French Knot

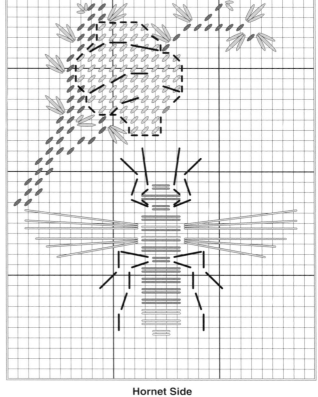

Hornet Side
29 holes x 37 holes
Cut 1

Rooster

Design by Alida Macor

Skill Level

Beginner

Size

Fits boutique-style tissue box

Materials

- 1½ sheets 7-count plastic canvas
- Medium weight yarn as listed in color key
- #16 tapestry needle

Project Note

The flower, heart, triangle and inverted triangle symbols designate Continental Stitches.

Instructions

1. Cut plastic canvas according to graphs (page 74).

2. Stitch pieces following graphs, working medium blue Straight Stitches as part of the background stitches.

3. When background stitching is completed, work tangerine Straight Stitch at beak.

4. For tail feathers, use 2-ply 12-inch (30.5cm) lengths yarn to work Lark's Head Knots where indicated at top of medium blue Straight

Stitches. Trim tail feathers a bit longer than the medium blue Straight Stitches under them.

5. Using cream throughout, Overcast inside edges of top and bottom edges of sides. Whipstitch sides together, then Whipstitch sides to top. ■

Graphs on page 74

Bow-Tie Kitty

Design by Kathy Wirth

Skill Level

Beginner

Size

Fits boutique-style tissue box

Materials

- 1½ sheets stiff 7-count plastic canvas
- Red Heart Classic Art. E267 medium weight yarn as listed in color key
- Red Heart Super Saver Art. E300 medium weight yarn as listed in color key
- Red Heart Kids Art. E711 medium weight yarn as listed in color key
- #16 tapestry needle

Instructions

1. Cut plastic canvas according to graphs.

2. Stitch pieces following graphs, working uncoded areas on white background with yellow Continental

Stitches and uncoded areas on yellow background with yellow Reverse Continental Stitches.

3. When background stitching is completed, work black French Knots for eyes. Using 2 plies black, work Backstitches for mouths.

4. Using turqua throughout, Overcast inside edges on top. Whipstitch sides together, then Whipstitch sides to top. Overcast bottom edges. ■

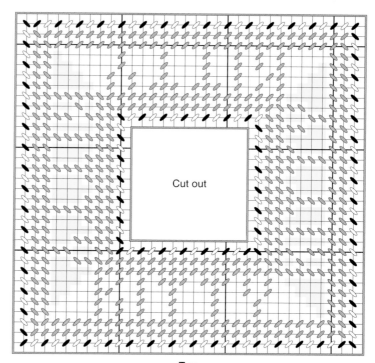

Top
33 holes x 33 holes
Cut 1

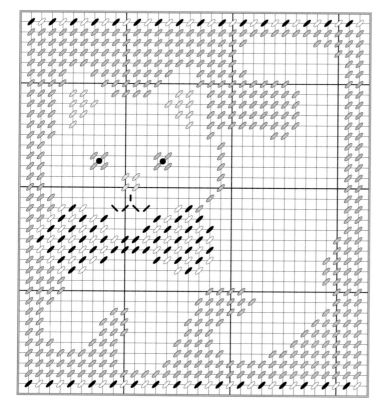

Side
33 holes x 37 holes
Cut 4

COLOR KEY

Yards	Medium Weight Yarn
9 (8.3m)	☐ White #1
11 (10.1m)	■ Black #12
16 (14.7m)	☐ Orange #245
33 (30.2m)	☐ Turqua #512
2 (1.9m)	☐ Pink #737
40 (36.6m)	Uncoded areas on white background are yellow #2230 Continental Stitches
	Uncoded areas on yellow background are yellow #2230 Reverse Continental Stitches
	╱ Black #12 (2-ply) Backstitch
	● Black #12 French Knot

Color numbers given are for Red Heart Classic Art. E267, Super Saver Art. E300 and Kids Art. E711 medium weight yarn.

Elephant

Design by Gina Woods

Skill Level

Beginner

Size

Fits boutique-style
tissue box

Materials

- 2 sheets clear 7-count
  plastic canvas
- Medium weight yarn as
  listed in color key
- 6-strand embroidery floss
  as listed in color key
- #16 tapestry needle
- 8 (1-inch/2.5cm) lengths
  white Venice lace each
  with 3 (¼-inch/7mm)
  hearts *or* small amount
  white 2mm craft foam
- 6 (9 x 12mm) red pearl
  heart pony beads
- Craft glue for nonporous
  materials
- Hot-glue gun

Instructions

1. Cut plastic canvas according to graphs (this page and page 54). If not using lace, cut 24 toenails from white craft foam.

2. Stitch and Overcast elephant pieces following graphs working uncoded areas with light gray Continental Stitches.

3. Stitch tissue holder pieces following graphs, working uncoded areas with light pink Continental Stitches.

4. When background stitching is completed work black yarn and black floss embroidery on elephant bodies. Embroider stems, leaves and flowers on sides and top with spring green and dark pink as indicated.

5. Using photo as a guide through step 8, and hot glue through step 6, adhere trunks to bodies. Glue lace or craft foam toenails to bottom of legs.

6. Glue ears to topper sides where indicated with green lines; glue bodies in place where indicated with blue lines.

7. Using dark pink throughout, Whipstitch sides together, then Whipstitch sides to top. Overcast inside edges of top and bottom edges of sides.

8. Use craft glue to adhere heart pony beads to top and elephant bodies where indicated. ∎

Elephant Ear
13 holes x 11 holes
Cut 8

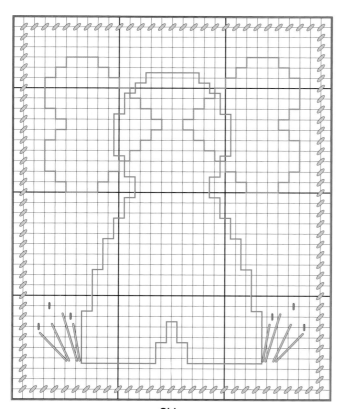

Side
30 holes x 37 holes
Cut 4

COLOR KEY	
Yards	**Medium Weight Yarn**
30 (27.5m)	▨ Bright pink
10 (9.2m)	■ Dark pink
56 (51.3m)	Uncoded areas on topper pieces are light pink Continental Stitches
36 (33m)	Uncoded areas on elephant pieces are light gray Continental Stitches
	⁄ Light gray Overcast
	⁄ Dark pink Straight Stitch
2 (1.9m)	⁄ Spring green Straight Stitch
1 (1m)	⁄ Black Straight Stitch
	⌀ Spring green Lazy Daisy Stitch
	6-Strand Embroidery Floss
1 (1m)	⁄ Black Straight Stitch
	♥ Attach heart pony bead

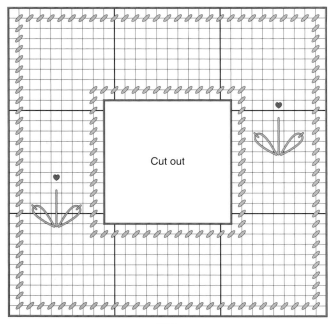

Top
30 holes x 30 holes
Cut 1

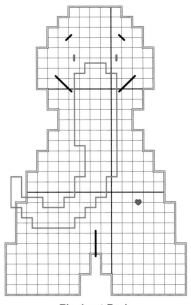

Elephant Body
17 holes x 28 holes
Cut 4

Elephant Toenail
Cut 24 from
white craft foam

COLOR KEY	
Yards	**Medium Weight Yarn**
30 (27.5m)	Bright pink
10 (9.2m)	Dark pink
56 (51.3m)	Uncoded areas on topper pieces are light pink Continental Stitches
36 (33m)	Uncoded areas on elephant pieces are light gray Continental Stitches
	Light gray Overcast
	Dark pink Straight Stitch
2 (1.9m)	Spring green Straight Stitch
1 (1m)	Black Straight Stitch
	Spring green Lazy Daisy Stitch
	6-Strand Embroidery Floss
1 (1m)	Black Straight Stitch
	Attach heart pony bead

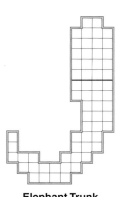

Elephant Trunk
10 holes x 16 holes
Cut 4

Betsy Bear

Design by Debra Arch

Skill Level

Intermediate

Size

Fits boutique-style tissue box

Materials

- 1 artist-size sheet 7-count plastic canvas
- 3 (6-inch) Uniek QuickShape plastic canvas hearts
- Red Heart Plush Art. E719 medium weight yarn as listed in color key
- #16 tapestry needle
- 2 (³⁄₈-inch/9mm) round black beads or buttons
- ⁷⁄₈-inch (22mm) round black shank button
- 9 inches (22.9cm) 1-inch/25mm-wide sheer cream ribbon
- Button shank remover or wire cutter
- Hot-glue gun

Instructions

1. Cut plastic canvas according to graphs (pages 56, 57 and 75), cutting away gray areas on hearts.

2. Following graphs throughout and using 2 strands yarn through step 6, stitch and Overcast muzzle. Stitch all remaining pieces. Overcast inside edges on side/top.

3. With right sides facing, Whipstitch ear back pieces to front edge of side/top where indicated on graphs with blue brackets.

4. With wrong sides facing, Whipstitch back to opposite side of side/top, easing as necessary to fit.

5. With right sides facing, Whipstitch ear front pieces to head where indicated on graphs with red brackets.

6. With wrong sides facing, Whipstitch head to front edge of side/top, Whipstitching around ears and easing as necessary to fit.

Finishing

1. Use photo as a guide throughout finishing. Center and glue muzzle to head, making sure bottom edges are even.

2. For nose, cut shank from ⅞-inch (22mm) black button, then glue nose to muzzle where indicated on graph.

3. For eyes, glue ⅜-inch (9mm) beads or buttons to head above muzzle.

4. Wrap 1 strand taupe five times around three fingers. Remove from fingers and tie another length taupe around center for hair tuft. Glue tuft to center top edge of head.

5. Form a four-loop bow from sheer ribbon; glue to head near tuft. Trim ends as desired. ∎

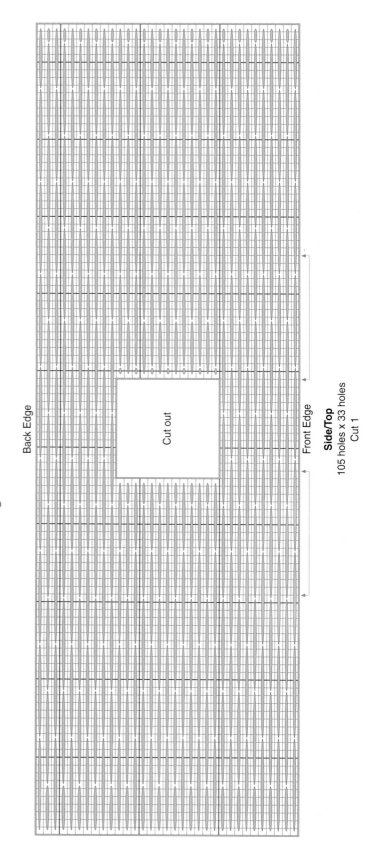

Back Edge

Cut out

Front Edge

Side/Top
105 holes x 33 holes
Cut 1

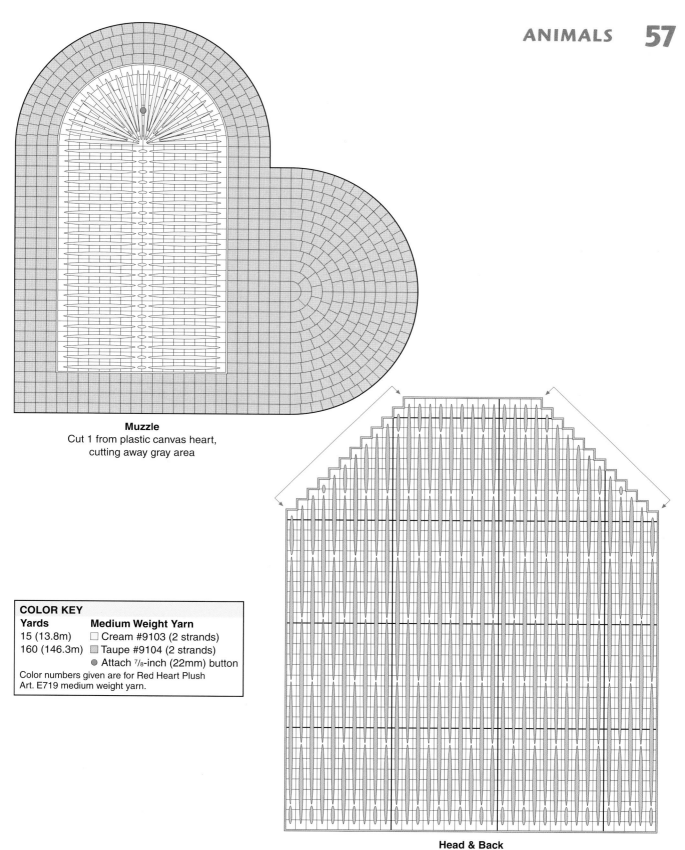

Muzzle
Cut 1 from plastic canvas heart,
cutting away gray area

COLOR KEY

Yards	Medium Weight Yarn
15 (13.8m)	☐ Cream #9103 (2 strands)
160 (146.3m)	☐ Taupe #9104 (2 strands)
	● Attach $7/8$-inch (22mm) button

Color numbers given are for Red Heart Plush
Art. E719 medium weight yarn.

Head & Back
35 holes x 42 holes
Cut 2

Graphs continued on page 75

Polka-Dot Chicken

Design by Kathy Wirth

Skill Level

Intermediate

Size

Fits boutique-style tissue box

Materials

- 2 sheets stiff 7-count plastic canvas
- Red Heart Super Saver Art. E300 medium weight yarn as listed in color key
- Red Heart Kids Art. E711 medium weight yarn as listed in color key
- #16 tapestry needle

Instructions

1. Cut plastic canvas according to graphs.

2. Following graphs through step 6, stitch sides, working uncoded areas with black Continental Stitches. Do not stitch blue Whipstitch lines at this time.

3. When background stitching is completed, work linen and yellow Straight Stitches.

4. Stitch top, working uncoded areas on white background with black Continental Stitches and uncoded areas on blue background with black Reverse Continental Stitches.

5. Stitch wings. Overcast around side and bottom edges from blue dot to blue dot. Using yellow, Whipstitch top edges of wings to sides along blue Whipstitch lines.

6. Overcast inside edges on top. Whipstitch sides together, then Whipstitch sides to top. Overcast bottom edges. ■

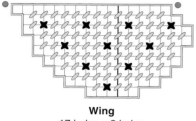

Wing
17 holes x 9 holes
Cut 4

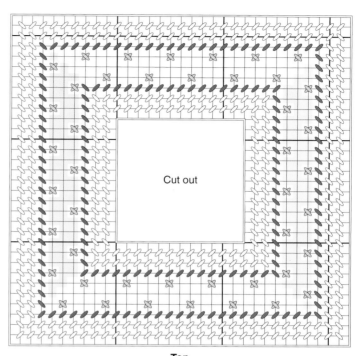

Cut out

Top
32 holes x 32 holes
Cut 1

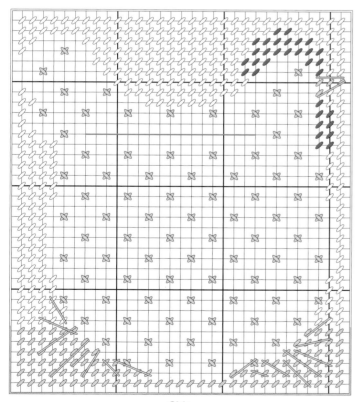

Side
32 holes x 37 holes
Cut 4

COLOR KEY	
Yards	**Medium Weight Yarn**
27 (24.7m)	☐ White #311
45 (41.2m)	■ Black #312
6 (5.5m)	■ Cherry red #319
12 (11m)	☐ Linen #330
23 (21.1m)	☐ Yellow #2230
40 (36.6m)	Uncoded areas on white background are black #312 Continental Stitches Uncoded areas on blue background are black #312 Reverse Continental Stitches
⁄	Linen #330 Straight Stitch
⁄	Yellow #2230 Straight Stitch

Color numbers given are for Red Heart Super Saver Art. E300 and Kids Art. E711 medium weight yarn.

Kitty

Design by Christina Laws

Skill Level

Beginner

Size

Fits family-size tissue box

Materials

- 3 sheets 7-count plastic canvas
- Medium weight yarn as listed in color key
- #16 tapestry needle
- Hot-glue gun

Instructions

1. Cut plastic canvas according to graphs (pages 61, 62 and 63). Cut two 34-hole x 28-hole pieces for sides.

2. Stitch sides with light gray Continental Stitches. Following graphs throughout all stitching, stitch and Overcast paws. Stitch back and top.

3. Stitch kitty front, working uncoded areas with light gray Continental Stitches. Reverse kitty backing; stitch outside red lines only,

using Reverse Continental Stitches and working ears with light gray instead of pink.

4. When background stitching on kitty front is completed, use 2 plies black to work Backstitches and a full strand white to Straight Stitch eye highlights.

5. Whipstitch top to sides. Using light gray, Whipstitch right side and top to right side of kitty backing along red lines. Whipstitch top and sides to back.

6. Whipstitch kitty front to kitty backing around all edges, Whipstitching left side to kitty front and backing while stitching, working through all three layers.

7. Overcast all remaining edges.

8. Using photo as a guide, glue paws to kitty front, making sure bottom edges are even. ■

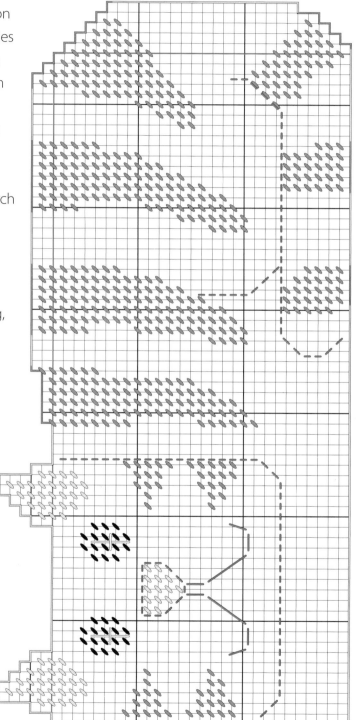

Kitty Front & Backing
70 holes x 33 holes
Cut 2
Stitch front as graphed
Reverse backing and stitch outside red lines with Reverse Continental Stitches, replacing pink on ears with light gray

COLOR KEY
Yards	Medium Weight Yarn
70 (64m)	☐ Light gray
10 (9.2m)	■ Dark gray
3 (2.8m)	☐ White
2 (1.9m)	☐ Pink
1 (1m)	■ Black

Uncoded areas on kitty are light gray Continental Stitches
⁄ White Straight Stitch
⁄ Black (2-ply) Backstitch

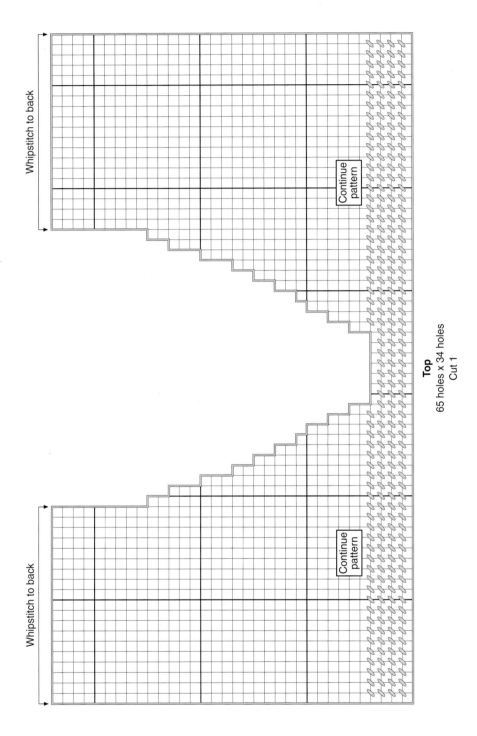

Whipstitch to back

Whipstitch to back

Continue pattern

Continue pattern

Top
65 holes x 34 holes
Cut 1

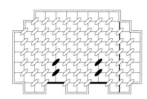

Paw
12 holes x 8 holes
Cut 2

COLOR KEY

Yards	Medium Weight Yarn
70 (64m)	Light gray
10 (9.2m)	Dark gray
3 (2.8m)	White
2 (1.9m)	Pink
1 (1m)	Black

Uncoded areas on
kitty are light gray
Continental Stitches
⁄ White Straight Stitch
⁄ Black (2-ply) Backstitch

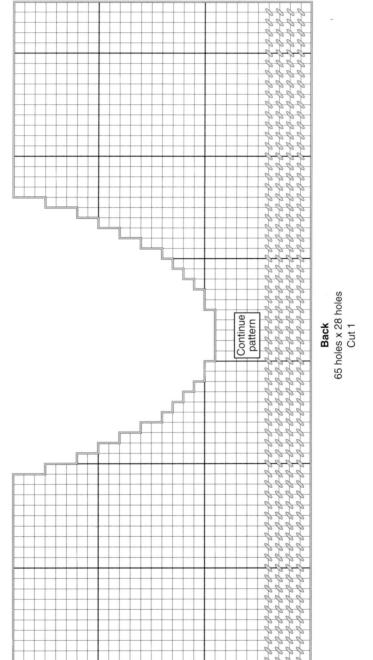

Back
65 holes x 28 holes
Cut 1

Continue
pattern

Under the Sea

Design by Kathy Wirth

Skill Level

Intermediate

Size

Fits family-size tissue box

Materials

- 2 sheets stiff 7-count plastic canvas
- Red Heart Classic Art. E267 medium weight yarn as listed in color key

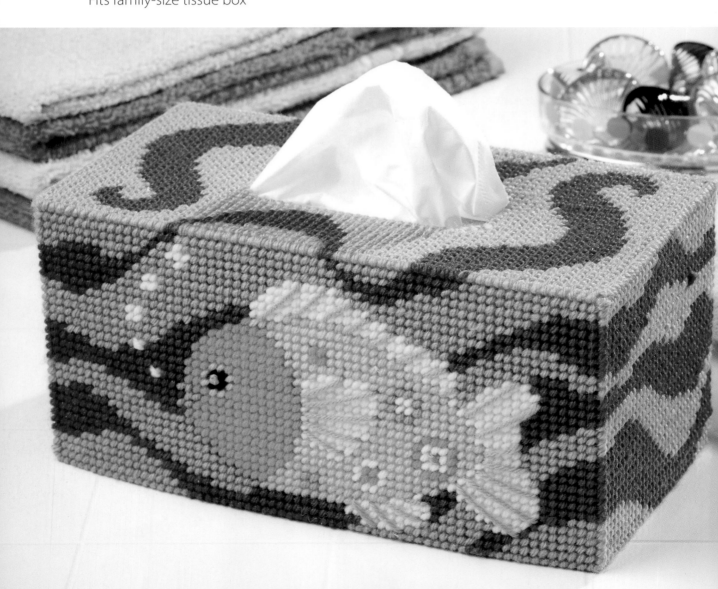

- Red Heart Super Saver Art. E300 medium weight yarn as listed in color key
- Red Heart Kids Art. E711 medium weight yarn as listed in color key
- #16 tapestry needle

Instructions

1. Cut plastic canvas according to graphs (this page and pages 66 and 67).

2. Stitch pieces following graphs, working Continental Stitches in uncoded areas as follows: white background with jade and yellow background with yellow.

3. When background stitching is completed, work French Knots on eyes and Straight Stitches on fins with spring green.

4. Using jade, Overcast inside edges on top; Whipstitch sides to ends. Whipstitch sides and ends to top with jade and blue. Overcast bottom edges. ■

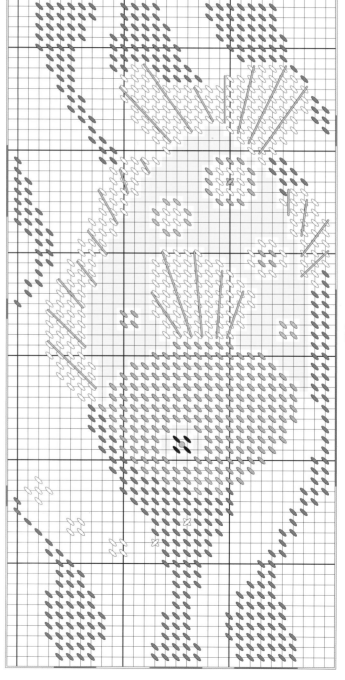

Side
65 holes x 31 holes
Cut 2

COLOR KEY	
Yards	**Medium Weight Yarn**
15 (13.8m)	☐ White #1
1 (1m)	■ Black #12
8 (7.4m)	▨ Tangerine #253
5 (4.6m)	▨ Spring green #672
51 (46.7m)	■ Blue #2845
40 (36.6m)	Uncoded areas on yellow background are yellow #2230 Continental Stitches
62 (56.7m)	Uncoded areas on white background are jade #2680 Continental Stitches
	╱ Jade #2680 Overcast and Whipstitch
	╱ Spring green #672 Straight Stitch
	◦ Spring green #672 French Knot

Color numbers given are for Red Heart Classic Art. E267, Super Saver Art. E300 and Kids Art. E711 medium weight yarn.

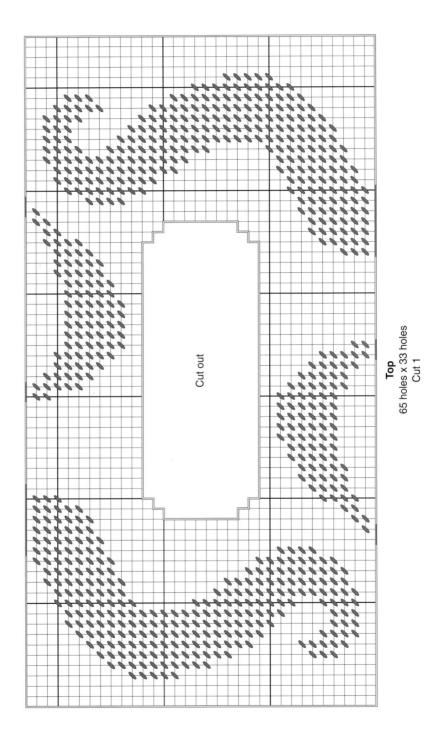

Top
65 holes x 33 holes
Cut 1

Cut out

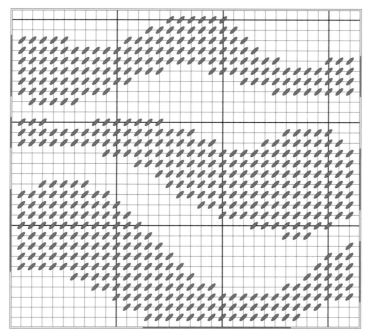

End
33 holes x 31 holes
Cut 2

COLOR KEY

Yards	Medium Weight Yarn
15 (13.8m)	☐ White #1
1 (1m)	■ Black #12
8 (7.4m)	▨ Tangerine #253
5 (4.6m)	▨ Spring green #672
51 (46.7m)	■ Blue #2845
40 (36.6m)	Uncoded areas on yellow background are yellow #2230 Continental Stitches
62 (56.7m)	Uncoded areas on white background are jade #2680 Continental Stitches
	╱ Jade #2680 Overcast and Whipstitch
	╱ Spring green #672 Straight Stitch
	● Spring green #672 French Knot

Color numbers given are for Red Heart Classic Art. E267, Super Saver Art. E300 and Kids Art. E711 medium weight yarn.

Desktop Pets

Design by Janelle Giese

Skill Level
Advanced

Size
Fits boutique-style tissue box
With Pockets: 8⅝ inches W x 5⅞ inches H x
5³⁄₁₆ inches D (21.9cm x 15cm x 13.2cm)

Materials
- 2 sheets clear stiff 7-count plastic canvas
- ⅔ sheet royal blue 7-count plastic canvas
- Red Heart Classic Art. E267 medium weight yarn as listed in color key
- Red Heart Super Saver Art. E300 and Art. E301 medium weight yarn as listed in color key
- Red Heart Kids Art. E711 medium weight yarn as listed in color key
- #3 pearl cotton as listed in color key
- #5 pearl cotton as listed in color key
- #16 tapestry needle

Project Notes
The diamond, flower, heart, star, square and triangle symbols designate Continental Stitches.

Triangles with the top pointing in a northwest direction are Reverse Continental Stitches.
Use a full strand (4 plies) yarn unless otherwise instructed.

Instructions
1. Cut front, back, pocket fronts, pocket sides, lid top and one base from clear stiff plastic canvas according to graphs (pages 70, 71, 72 and 73).

2. From royal blue plastic canvas, cut one base liner and four 30-hole x 14-hole pieces for lid lips. Base, base liner and lid lips will remain unstitched.

3. Stitch tissue holder front and back following graph, working uncoded areas with Continental Stitches as follows: peach background with copper, blue background with warm brown, white background with amethyst, green background with paddy green, yellow background with yellow #2230.

4. When background stitching is completed, follow color key and graph to stitch embroidery, working yarn stitches before pearl cotton stitches. For eye highlights, bring white pearl cotton up in hole at top end of yarn stitch, then down, piercing through yarn stitch where indicated.

5. Stitch tissue holder sides, pocket fronts, pocket sides and lid top following graphs, leaving bars indicated with red Whipstitch line on lid top unworked at this time. Overcast inside edges of lid top.

Assembly

1. Using amethyst throughout assembly, Whipstitch lid lips together along short edges; Overcast bottom edges.

2. Whipstitch top edges of lid lips to lid top along red Whipstitch line using stitches indicated on lid top, beginning with amethyst Cross Stitches and finishing with jade Continental Stitches.

3. Whipstitch two pocket sides together. Repeat with remaining pocket sides, creating four pairs. Whipstitch one pair to each side of pocket front pieces.

4. Place pockets next to tissue holder sides

(see photo). Whipstitch tissue holder front and back to tissue holder sides, attaching pocket sides to corners where indicated with brackets while Whipstitching, working through all three layers.

5. Place base pieces together with royal blue on top. Working through all three layers, Whipstitch bottom edges of tissue holder to base pieces where indicated with blue lines.

6. Working through all three layers, Whipstitch pockets to base pieces where indicated with red lines, Whipstitching remaining edges of base pieces together while working your way around.

7. Overcast all remaining edges. ■

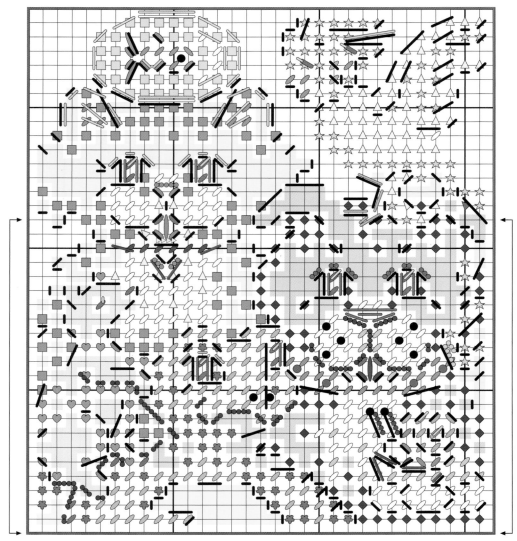

Tissue Holder Front & Back
32 holes x 37 holes
Cut 2 from clear stiff

COLOR KEY

Yards	Medium Weight Yarn
4 (3.7m)	⬠ White #1
2 (1.9m)	✎ Black #12
3 (2.8m)	☆ Yellow #230
1 (1m)	⬠ Sea coral #246
3 (2.8m)	△ Maize #261
4 (3.7m)	◆ Bronze #286
4 (3.7m)	▼ Copper #289 Reverse Continental Stitch
3 (2.8m)	◼ Gold #321
1 (1m)	⬠ Tan #334
2 (1.9m)	◣ Warm brown #336
1 (1m)	♥ Cafe #360
34 (31.1m)	✖ Amethyst #588
2 (1.9m)	✿ Emerald green #676
1 (1m)	⬠ Grenadine #730
2 (1.9m)	⬠ Orange #2252
1 (1m)	✎ Red #2390
39 (35.7m)	⬠ Lime #2652
34 (31.1m)	◻ Jade #2680
	Uncoded areas on peach background are copper #289 Continental Stitches
	Uncoded areas on blue background are warm brown #336 Continental Stitches
	Uncoded areas on white background are amethyst #588 Continental Stitches
1 (1m)	Uncoded areas on green background are paddy green #686 Continental Stitches
6 (5.5m)	Uncoded areas on yellow background are yellow #2230 Continental Stitches
	⬠ White #1 Straight Stitch (fishbowl)
	✎ Black #12 Straight Stitch (dog's nose, bird's eyes)
	⬠ Yellow #230 Straight Stitch (bird's ears; cat's eyelids and ears)
	⬠ Sea coral #246 Straight Stitch (bird's feet)
	✐ Copper #289 Straight Stitch (dog's eyelids)
1 (1m)	✎ Brown #328 (2-ply) Straight Stitch (dog's and turtle's eyes)
	✎ Emerald green #676 (2-ply) Straight Stitch (cat's eyes)
	✐ Grenadine #730 Straight Stitch (cat's nose and collar medallion)
	✐ Yellow #2230 Straight Stitch (bird's tail)
	✎ Red #2390 Straight Stitch (cat's collar medallion and crab's legs)
	✐ Red #2390 (2-ply) Straight Stitch (crab's antennae)
	⬠ Lime #2652 Straight Stitch (turtle's eyelids)
	⬤ Brown #328 French Knot (dog's collar)

#3 Pearl Cotton

3 (2.8m)	⬠ White Backstitch and Straight Stitch (eye highlights, cat's ears, fishbowl)
2 (1.9m)	✐ Black Backstitch and Straight Stitch

#5 Pearl Cotton

15 (13.8m)	✎ Black Backstitch and Straight Stitch
	⬤ Black French Knot (dog's muzzle, crab's eyes, fish's eye, turtle's nose)

Color numbers given are for Red Heart medium weight yarn: Classic Art. E267, Super Saver Art. E300 and Art. E301, and Kids Art. E711.

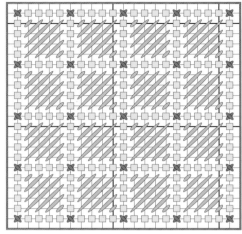

Pocket Front
22 holes x 22 holes
Cut 2 from clear stiff

Pocket Side
7 holes x 22 holes
Cut 8 from clear stiff

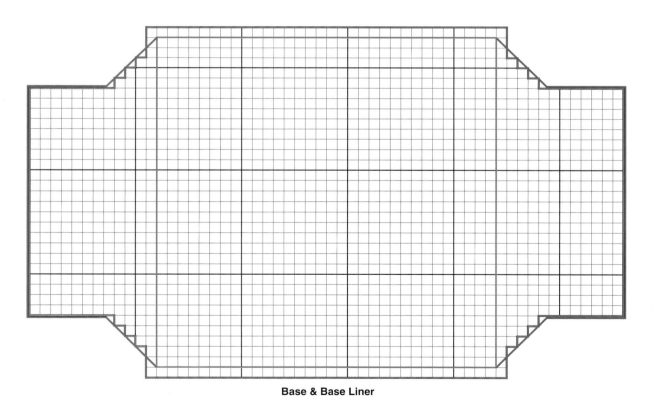

Base & Base Liner
56 holes x 34 holes
Cut 1 from clear stiff for base
Do not stitch
Cut 1 from royal blue for base liner
Do not stitch

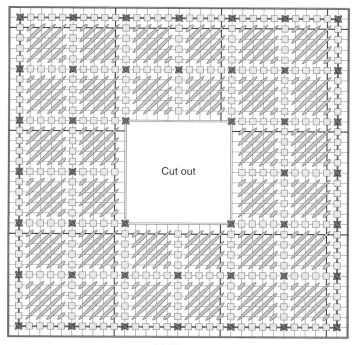

Lid Top
32 holes x 32 holes
Cut 1 from clear stiff

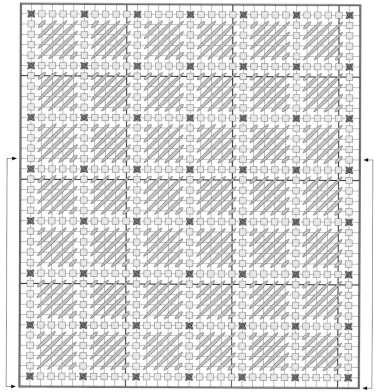

Tissue Holder Side
32 holes x 37 holes
Cut 2 from clear stiff

Continued from page 49

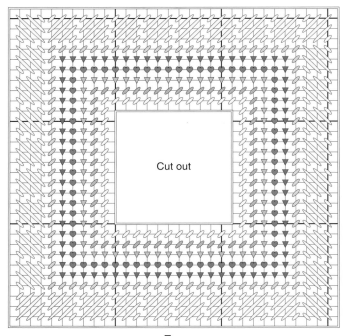

Top
31 holes x 31 holes
Cut 1

COLOR KEY	
Yards	**Medium Weight Yarn**
56 (51.3m)	⬭ Cream
14 (12.9m)	▼ Medium blue
8 (7.4m)	⬭ Medium brown
8 (7.4m)	⬭ Bright green
5 (4.6m)	▽ Tangerine
5 (4.6m)	♥ Bright rose
5 (4.6m)	⬭ Aqua
2 (1.9m)	✿ Purple
2 (1.9m)	△ Medium yellow
1 (1m)	⬭ Black (2 plies)
	⬭ Medium blue Straight Stitch
	⬭ Tangerine Straight Stitch
	● Medium blue (2-ply) Lark's Head Knot
	● Bright green (2-ply) Lark's Head Knot
	○ Aqua (2-ply) Lark's Head Knot
	● Purple (2-ply) Lark's Head Knot

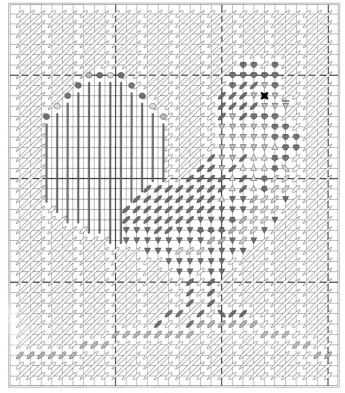

Side
31 holes x 37 holes
Cut 4

Continued from page 57

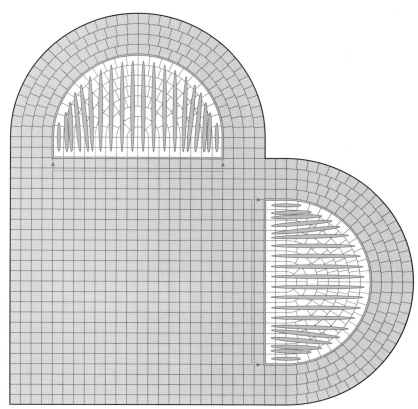

Ear Back Pieces
Cut 2 from plastic canvas heart,
cutting away gray area

COLOR KEY	
Yards	**Medium Weight Yarn**
15 (13.8m)	☐ Cream #9103 (2 strands)
160 (146.3m)	☐ Taupe #9104 (2 strands)
	● Attach 7/8-inch (22mm) button

Color numbers given are for Red Heart Plush
Art. E719 medium weight yarn.

Ear Front Pieces
Cut 2 from plastic canvas heart,
cutting away gray area

Florals

Light & Shadow Roses

Design by Angie Arickx

Skill Level

Beginner

Size

Fits boutique-style tissue box

Materials

- 1½ sheets 7-count plastic canvas
- Red Heart Super Saver Art. E300 medium weight yarn as listed in color key
- Red Heart Classic Art. E267 medium weight yarn as listed in color key
- #16 tapestry needle

Instructions

1. Cut plastic canvas according to graphs.

2. Stitch pieces following graphs, working Continental Stitches in uncoded areas as follows: white background with white, gray background with black.

3. Using black, Overcast inside edges of top and bottom edges of sides. Whipstitch sides together, then Whipstitch sides to top. ■

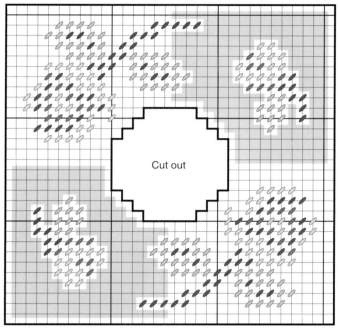

Top
31 holes x 31 holes
Cut 1

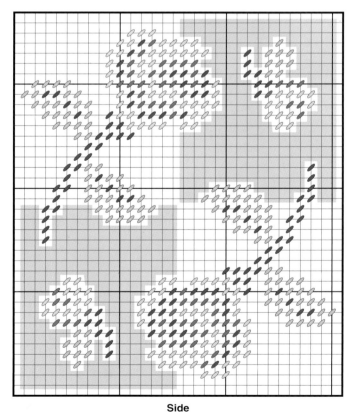

Side
31 holes x 37 holes
Cut 4

COLOR KEY

Yards	Medium Weight Yarn
4 (3.7m)	■ Cherry red #319
7 (6.5m)	■ Paddy green #368
5 (4.6m)	■ Burgundy #376
9 (8.3m)	□ Hot red #390
9 (8.3m)	▨ Emerald #676
22 (20.2m)	Uncoded areas on white background are white #311 Continental Stitches
33 (30.2m)	Uncoded areas on gray background are black #312 Continental Stitches
	╱ Black #312 Overcast and Whipstitch

Color numbers given are for Red Heart Super Saver Art. E300 and Classic Art. E267 medium weight yarn.

Flowery Bronze

Design by Angie Arickx

Skill Level

Beginner

Size

Fits family-style tissue box

Materials

- 1½ sheets 7-count plastic canvas
- Red Heart Classic Art. E267 medium weight yarn as listed in color key
- #16 tapestry needle

Instructions

1. Cut plastic canvas according to graphs (pages 81 and 93).

2. Stitch pieces following graphs.

3. Using bronze, Overcast inside edges of top and bottom edges of sides and ends. Whipstitch sides to ends, then Whipstitch sides and ends to top. ■

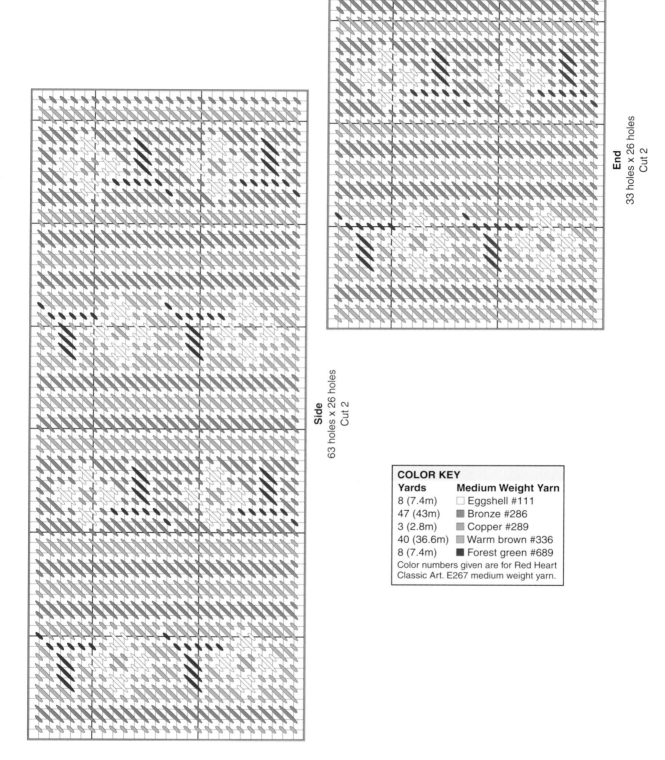

End
33 holes x 26 holes
Cut 2

Side
63 holes x 26 holes
Cut 2

COLOR KEY

Yards	Medium Weight Yarn
8 (7.4m)	☐ Eggshell #111
47 (43m)	■ Bronze #286
3 (2.8m)	■ Copper #289
40 (36.6m)	■ Warm brown #336
8 (7.4m)	■ Forest green #689

Color numbers given are for Red Heart
Classic Art. E267 medium weight yarn.

Graphs continued on page 93

Flower Garden

Design by Glenda Chamberlain

Skill Level

Beginner

Size

Fits regular-size tissue box

Materials

- 2 sheets 7-count plastic canvas
- Red Heart Super Saver Art. E300 medium weight yarn as listed in color key
- 6-strand embroidery floss as listed in color key
- #16 tapestry needle
- Decorative buttons: 2 hearts, 2 dragonflies, 4 bumblebees
- Button shank remover or wire cutters
- Hot-glue gun

Instructions

1. Cut plastic canvas according to graphs (this page and page 94).

2. Stitch pieces following graphs, working uncoded areas with hunter green Continental Stitches.

3. When background stitching is completed, work dark orchid and black yarn French Knots for centers of flowers.

4. Using black floss, outline fence and work detail on birdhouses.

5. Using hunter green, Overcast inside edges of top and bottom edges of sides and ends. Whipstitch sides to ends, then Whipstitch sides and ends to top.

6. Using photo as a guide through step 7, glue roof to birdhouse, then glue one birdhouse to each side.

7. Cut shanks off buttons; glue one heart button to center of each birdhouse. Glue remaining buttons to top and sides as desired. ■

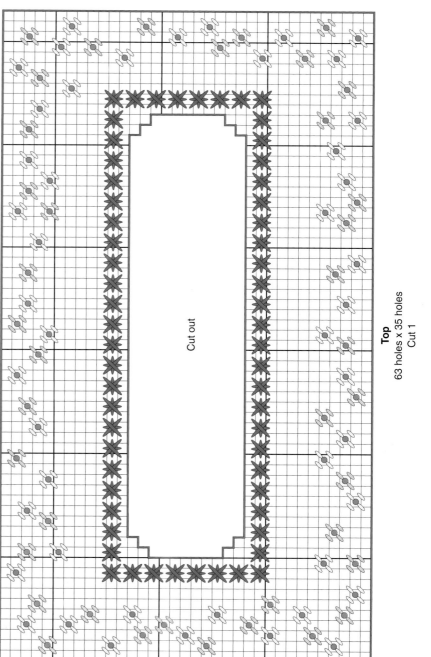

Top
63 holes x 35 holes
Cut 1

Cut out

COLOR KEY	
Yards	**Medium Weight Yarn**
12 (11m)	■ Black #312
20 (18.3m)	□ Soft white #316
26 (23.8m)	□ Cornmeal #320
4 (3.7m)	■ Coffee #365
4 (3.7m)	□ Light blue #381
35 (32m)	■ Hunter green #389
26 (23.8m)	□ Orchid #530
	Uncoded areas are hunter green #389 Continental Stitches
	● Black #312 French Knot
10 (9.2m)	● Dark orchid #776 French Knot
	6-Strand Embroidery Floss
12 (11m)	✏ Black Backstitch and Straight Stitch
Color numbers given are for Red Heart Super Saver Art. E300 medium weight yarn.	

Graphs continued on page 94

Daisies

Design by Kathy Wirth

Skill Level

Beginner

Size

Fits boutique-style tissue box

Materials

- 2 sheets 7-count plastic canvas
- Red Heart Classic Art. E267 medium weight yarn as listed in color key
- Red Heart Super Saver Art. E300 medium weight yarn as listed in color key
- Red Heart Kids Art. E711 medium weight yarn as listed in color key
- #16 tapestry needle

Instructions

1. Cut plastic canvas according to graphs.

2. Stitch pieces following graphs, working uncoded areas on white background with soft navy Continental Stitches. Do not stitch areas shaded with pink and blue.

3. Overcast flowers with white. Place one flower on each side, matching pink shaded areas. Work four lime Continental Stitches through both layers to attach flowers to sides.

4. Whipstitch corners to sides, easing as necessary to fit. Overcast top and bottom edges of sides with delft blue; Overcast top and bottom edges of corners with lime. ■

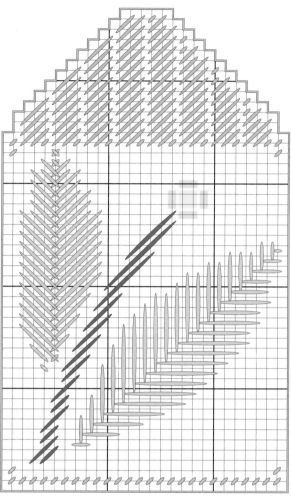

Side
27 holes x 47 holes
Cut 4

Corner
7 holes x 51 holes
Cut 4

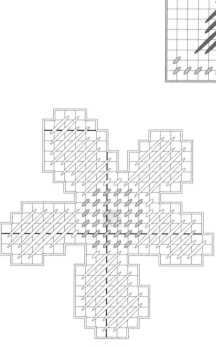

Flower
20 holes x 22 holes
Cut 4

COLOR KEY

Yards	Medium Weight Yarn
18 (16.5m)	☐ White #1
4 (3.7m)	◼ Emerald green #676
25 (22.9m)	◻ Delft blue #885
25 (22.9m)	◻ Lime #2652
38 (34.8m)	Uncoded areas on white background are soft navy #853 Continental Stitches

Color numbers given are for Red Heart Classic Art. E267, Super Saver Art. E300 and Kids Art. E711 medium weight yarn.

Strawflowers

Design by Deborah Scheblein

Skill Level

Beginner

Size

Fits boutique-style tissue box

Materials

- 1½ sheets 7-count plastic canvas
- Medium weight yarn as listed in color key
- #16 tapestry needle
- 8 (¼-inch/6mm) yellow pompoms
- 4 (1⅝-inch/4.1cm-long, including antennae) scrapbooking or sticker bees
- Hot-glue gun

Instructions

1. Cut plastic canvas according to graphs.

2. Stitch pieces following graphs, working uncoded backgrounds with light blue Continental Stitches.

3. When background stitching is completed, Straight Stitch flower petals and center vein on leaves,

working two sides with purple and bright pink flower petals as graphed. Stitch remaining two sides, replacing purple with royal blue and bright pink with bright orange.

4. Following graphs throughout, Overcast inside edges of top and bottom edges of sides. Whipstitch sides with royal blue and bright orange petals to sides with purple and bright pink petals. Whipstitch sides to top.

5. Glue yellow pompoms to center of flowers. Glue a bee to each side above shortest flower. ■

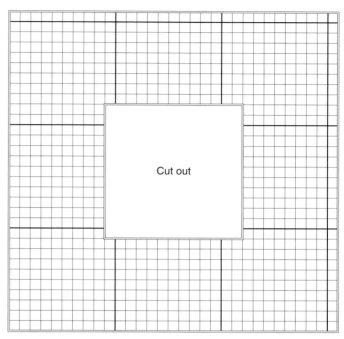

Top
31 holes x 31 holes
Cut 1

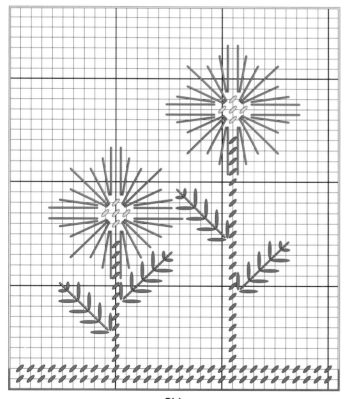

Side
31 holes x 37 holes
Cut 4
Stitch 2 as graphed
Stitch 2 replacing
purple with royal blue and
bright pink with bright orange

COLOR KEY

Yards	Medium Weight Yarn
11 (10.1m)	■ Christmas green
1 (1m)	☐ Yellow
74 (67.7m)	Uncoded areas are light blue Continental Stitches
	╱ Light blue Overcast and Whipstitch
	╱ Christmas green Straight Stitch
2 (1.9m)	╱ Purple Straight Stitch
2 (1.9m)	╱ Bright pink Straight Stitch
2 (1.9m)	Royal blue Straight Stitch
2 (1.9m)	Bright orange Straight Stitch

Wildflowers

Design by Gina Woods

Skill Level

Intermediate

Size

Fits boutique-style tissue box

Materials

- 2 sheets 7-count plastic canvas
- Medium weight yarn as listed in color key
- Caron Simply Soft medium weight yarn as listed in color key
- Caron Bliss bulky weight yarn as listed in color key
- DMC 6-strand embroidery floss as listed in color key
- #16 tapestry needle

Instructions

1. Cut plastic canvas according to graphs (pages 89 and 95).

2. Stitch pieces following graphs, working Continental Stitches in uncoded areas as follows: white background with lime (*top piece, bleeding heart*

and gentian blocks), blue background with pale blue (bluebonnet and shooting star blocks), green background with medium green (sunflower, wild rose and thistle blocks), yellow background with dark green (thistle block).

Embroidery

1. Bluebonnet blocks: Use two plies blue and royal blue yarn to work Lazy Daisy Stitches for bluebonnets. Work medium green Straight Stitches for stems. Work French Knots with snow bulky weight yarn, wrapping needle two times for top blooms and one time for bottom blooms.

2. Bleeding heart blocks: Work dark green Straight Stitches for leaf decorations. Using floss, work very dark mahogany Backstitches for stems and 12-plies white for Lazy Daisy Stitches.

3. Wild rose blocks: Work rose French Knots around center for petals.

4. Thistle blocks: Work medium green Backstitches and Straight Stitches for leaves and

Continued on page 95

COLOR KEY	
Yards	**Medium Weight Yarn**
24 (22m)	▨ Periwinkle
20 (18.3m)	☐ Pale blue
12 (11m)	■ Dark green
8 (7.4m)	▨ Medium purple
6 (5.5m)	■ Royal blue
4 (3.7m)	▨ Rose
4 (3.7m)	☐ Yellow
4 (3.7m)	▨ Yellow-orange
2 (1m)	■ Dark brown
1 (1m)	■ Burgundy
1 (1m)	▨ Rubine red #2718
24 (22m)	Uncoded areas on white background are lime Continental Stitches Uncoded areas on blue background are pale blue Continental Stitches
12 (11m)	Uncoded areas on green background are medium green Continental Stitches Uncoded areas on yellow background are dark green Continental Stitches
	⁄ Medium green Straight Stitch
	⁄ Dark green Straight Stitch
	◖ Royal blue (2-ply) Lazy Daisy Stitch
1 (1m)	◖ Blue (2-ply) Lazy Daisy Stitch
	◯ Rose French Knot
	Bulky Weight Yarn
2 (1.9m)	◯ Snow #0001 (2-wrap) French Knot
	◯ Snow #0001 (1-wrap) French Knot
	6-Strand Embroidery Floss
1 (1m)	⁄ Very dark mahogany #300 Backstitch
1 (1m)	⁄ Bright chartreuse #704 Straight Stitch
1 (1m)	◖ White (12-ply) Lazy Daisy Stitch
3 (2.8m)	◖ Light topaz #726 Lazy Daisy Stitch
3 (2.8m)	◖ Deep canary #972 Lazy Daisy Stitch

Color numbers given are for Caron Simply Soft medium weight yarn and Bliss bulky weight yarn, and DMC 6-strand embroidery floss.

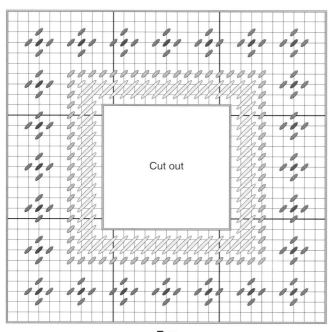

Top
30 holes x 30 holes
Cut 1

Slice of Watermelon

Design by Glenda Chamberlain

Skill Level

Intermediate

Size

Fits boutique-style tissue box

Materials

- 2 sheets 7-count plastic canvas
- Red Heart Super Saver Art. E300 medium weight yarn as listed in color key
- #16 tapestry needle
- Clean, dry watermelon seeds
- Hot-glue gun

Instructions

1. Cut plastic canvas according to graphs (this page and page 92).

2. Stitch front, back, top and sides following graphs, working uncoded areas on front, back and top with light raspberry Continental Stitches. Overcast opening on top with light raspberry.

3. Stitch and Overcast six small flowers as graphed. Stitch and Overcast five small flowers replacing petal pink with soft white and cornmeal with light raspberry.

4. Stitch and Overcast large flowers and leaves.

5. When background stitching is completed, work frosty green Straight Stitches on leaves and sides.

6. Following graphs, Whipstitch front and back to top, then Whipstitch front, back and top to sides, easing as necessary to fit. Overcast bottom edges.

7. Using photo as a guide, arrange flowers and leaves to front and top as desired; glue in place.

8. Glue watermelon seeds to front and back as desired. ∎

COLOR KEY	
Yards	**Medium Weight Yarn**
10 (9.2m)	☐ Soft white #316
5 (4.6m)	☐ Cornmeal #320
14 (12.9m)	☐ Petal pink #373
41 (37.5m)	■ Hunter green #389
17 (15.6m)	▨ Frosty green #661
48 (43.9m)	▨ Light raspberry #774
	Uncoded areas are light raspberry #774 Continental Stitches
	╱ Frosty green #661 Straight Stitch
Color numbers given are for Red Heart Super Saver Art. E300 medium weight yarn.	

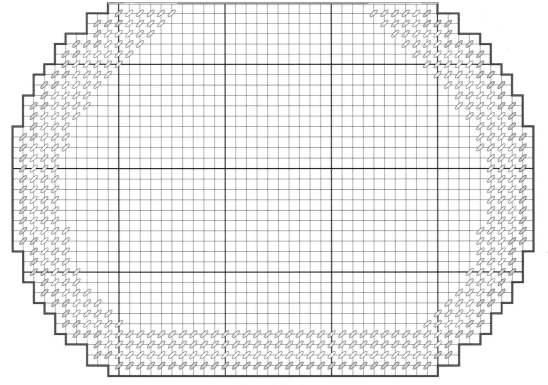

Front & Back
49 holes x 36 holes
Cut 2

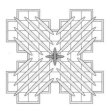

Large Flower
9 holes x 9 holes
Cut 4

Small Flower
7 holes x 7 holes
Cut 11
Stitch 6 as graphed
Stitch 5 replacing
petal pink with soft white
and cornmeal with
light raspberry

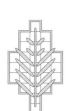

Leaf
5 holes x 9 holes
Cut 6

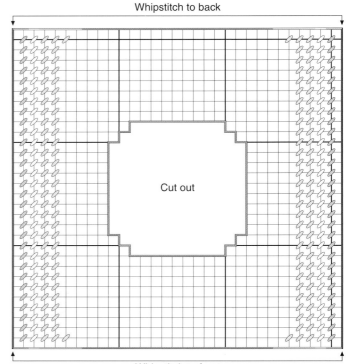

Whipstitch to back

Cut out

Whipstitch to front

Top
31 holes x 31 holes
Cut 1

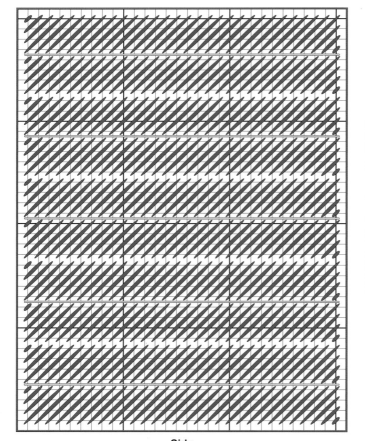

Side
31 holes x 41 holes
Cut 2

COLOR KEY	
Yards	**Medium Weight Yarn**
10 (9.2m)	☐ Soft white #316
5 (4.6m)	☐ Cornmeal #320
14 (12.9m)	☐ Petal pink #373
41 (37.5m)	■ Hunter green #389
17 (15.6m)	☐ Frosty green #661
48 (43.9m)	■ Light raspberry #774

Uncoded areas are light raspberry
#774 Continental Stitches

╱ Frosty green #661 Straight Stitch

Color numbers given are for Red Heart Super Saver
Art. E300 medium weight yarn.

Flowery Bronze

Continued from page 81

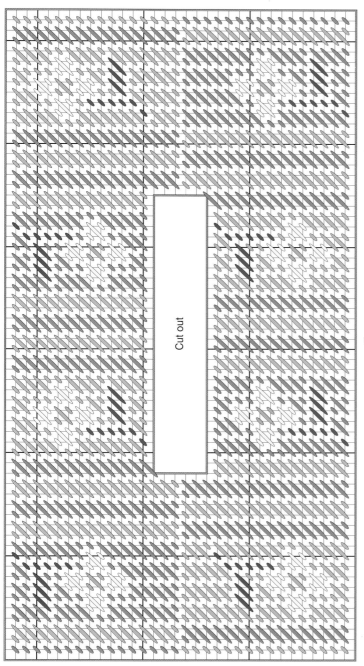

Top
63 holes x 33 holes
Cut 1

Cut out

COLOR KEY

Yards	Medium Weight Yarn
8 (7.4m)	☐ Eggshell #111
47 (43m)	▨ Bronze #286
3 (2.8m)	▨ Copper #289
40 (36.6m)	▨ Warm brown #336
8 (7.4m)	■ Forest green #689

Color numbers given are for Red Heart Classic Art. E267 medium weight yarn.

Continued from page 83

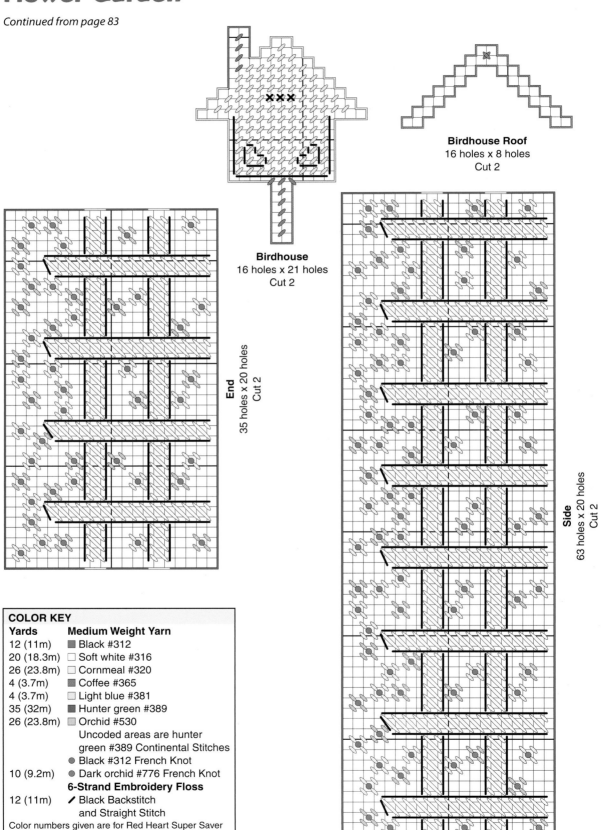

Birdhouse Roof
16 holes x 8 holes
Cut 2

Birdhouse
16 holes x 21 holes
Cut 2

End
35 holes x 20 holes
Cut 2

Side
63 holes x 20 holes
Cut 2

COLOR KEY

Yards	Medium Weight Yarn
12 (11m)	■ Black #312
20 (18.3m)	☐ Soft white #316
26 (23.8m)	☐ Cornmeal #320
4 (3.7m)	▨ Coffee #365
4 (3.7m)	☐ Light blue #381
35 (32m)	■ Hunter green #389
26 (23.8m)	☐ Orchid #530
	Uncoded areas are hunter green #389 Continental Stitches
	● Black #312 French Knot
10 (9.2m)	● Dark orchid #776 French Knot
	6-Strand Embroidery Floss
12 (11m)	╱ Black Backstitch and Straight Stitch

Color numbers given are for Red Heart Super Saver Art. E300 medium weight yarn.

Continued from page 89

stems. Use 1-ply bright chartreuse floss to work detail on thistle ball.

5. *Sunflower blocks*: Work light topaz Lazy Daisy Stitches around center for petals. Use deep canary to work Lazy Daisy Stitches between light topaz petals.

6. *Gentian blocks*: Work dark green Straight Stitches for leaves.

Assembly

1. Using periwinkle, Overcast inside edges on top and bottom edges of sides. Whipstitch sides together, then Whipstitch sides to top. ■

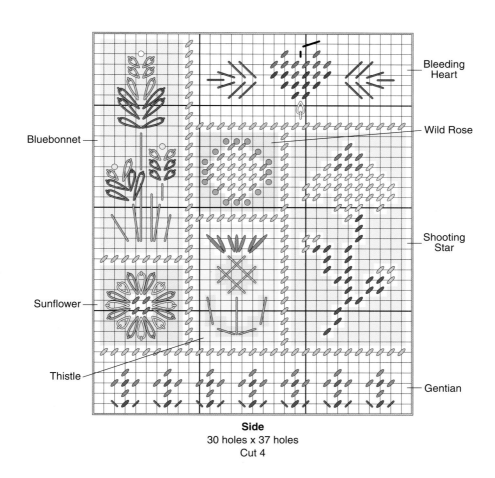

Side
30 holes x 37 holes
Cut 4

Bleeding Heart
Wild Rose
Shooting Star
Gentian
Bluebonnet
Sunflower
Thistle

Long Stitch

Fresh as a Daisy

Design by Debra Arch

Skill Level

Beginner

Size

Fits boutique-style tissue box
5-inch-tall cube (12.7cm)

Materials

- 1½ sheets 7-count plastic canvas
- Uniek Needloft plastic canvas yarn as listed in color key
- Kreinik ⅛-inch Ribbon as listed in color key
- #16 tapestry needle
- 85–100 lime glass E beads
- Hand-sewing needle
- Light green thread

Instructions

1. Cut plastic canvas according to graphs.

2. Stitch pieces following graphs, working uncoded areas with fern Continental Stitches and using 2 strands sunlight ribbon.

3. Using hand-sewing needle and light green thread, randomly attach 21–25 beads to center of each daisy on sides.

4. Following graphs, Overcast inside edges on top and bottom edges of sides. Whipstitch sides together, then Whipstitch sides to top. ∎

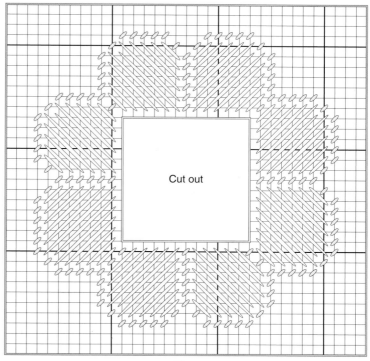

Top
34 holes x 34 holes
Cut 1

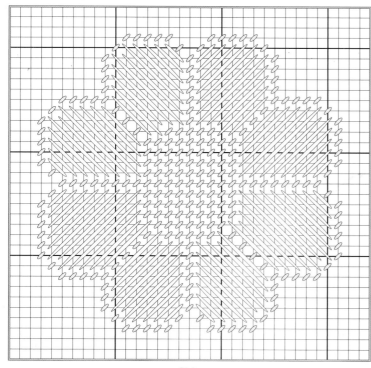

Side
34 holes x 34 holes
Cut 4

COLOR KEY

Yards	Plastic Canvas Yarn
35 (32m)	☐ White #41
50 (45.7m)	Uncoded areas are fern #23 Continental Stitches
	✎ Fern #23 Overcast and Whipstitch
	¹⁄₈-Inch Ribbon
50 (45.7m)	☐ Sunlight #9100 (2 strands)

Color numbers given are for Uniek Needloft plastic canvas yarn and Kreinik ¹⁄₈-inch Ribbon.

Vanity Tray

Design by Angie Arickx

Skill Level

Intermediate

Size

Fits family-style tissue box

Materials

- 2 sheets 7-count plastic canvas
- Red Heart Super Saver Art. E300 medium weight yarn as listed in color key
- #16 tapestry needle

Instructions

1. Cut plastic canvas according to graphs (pages 116, 117, 118 and 119).

2. Stitch pieces following graphs, working uncoded areas with medium purple Continental Stitches and leaving bars indicated with green lines on topper front unworked at this time.

3. Overcast inside edges on top. Overcast bottom edges of topper ends and back. Overcast top edges of tray front and ends.

4. Whipstitch topper front and back to topper ends. Whipstitch front, back and ends to top.

5. Whipstitch tray front to tray ends. Whipstitch front and ends to tray base.

6. Using medium purple, Whipstitch tray ends to bars indicated with green lines on topper front. Using pale plum, Whipstitch back edge of tray base to bottom edge of topper front, Overcasting remaining edges on topper front while Whipstitching. ∎

Graphs on pages 116–119

Flower Shop

Design by Nancy Dorman

Skill Level

Advanced

Size

Fits boutique-style tissue box

Materials

- 4 sheets clear 7-count plastic canvas
- ¼ sheet white 7-count plastic canvas
- ½ sheet 10-count plastic canvas
- ½ sheet 14-count plastic canvas
- Medium weight yarn as listed in color key
- Light weight yarn as listed in color key
- 6-strand embroidery floss as listed in color key
- Cloisonné metallic thread as listed in color key
- #16 tapestry needle
- ½ yard (0.5m) ⅛-inch/3mm-wide coordinating ribbon (optional) (sample used lavender and white)
- 3 inches (7.6cm) ¹⁄₁₆-inch/.2cm dowel
- White craft paint
- Small paintbrush
- Round toothpick
- Miniature artificial flowers
- Assorted trims and embellishments as desired (sample used flocked bear, watering can, small basket, miniature wreaths)
- Hot-glue gun

Project Note

Unless otherwise instructed, for background stitching, Overcasting and Whipstitching, use medium weight yarn with 7-count plastic canvas, light weight yarn with 10 count, and 6-strand embroidery floss with 14-count.

Shop & Base

1. Cut shop front, back, sides and base from clear 7-count plastic canvas according to graphs (pages 120, 121 and 124).

2. Stitch front, back, sides and base following graphs.

3. When background stitching is completed, use white light weight yarn to work Backstitches on back and side windows. Use blue-green medium weight yarn to embroider stems and leaves around bottom of back and sides. Do not work purple light weight yarn French Knots at this time.

4. Work black floss Backstitches for detail on front door. Work gold cloisonné thread French Knots for doorknobs.

5. Using either the regular Whipstitch or a Binding Stitch (page 124), stitch front and back to sides.

6. Using either the regular Overcast Stitch or Binding Stitch, stitch bottom edges of front, back and sides, and outside edges of base. Overcast top edges of front, back and sides, and inside edges of base.

Chimney & Roof

1. Cut chimney front, back and sides, chimney flowers, roof and roof trim pieces from clear 7-count plastic canvas according to graphs (pages 121 and 122).

2. Following graphs throughout, stitch chimney and roof pieces. Overcast chimney flowers; work bright yellow French Knots in centers.

3. Overcast bottom edges of chimney pieces. Overcast chimney opening on roof pieces. Overcast bottom edges of roof trim pieces from white dot to white dot.

4. Use white light weight yarn to work Straight Stitches on roof front and back trim pieces only and French Knots on all roof trim pieces.

5. Using either the regular Whipstitch, Overcast Stitch or a Binding Stitch through step 6, stitch chimney front and back to chimney sides. Stitch top edges of chimney.

6. Stitch top edges of roof pieces together. Stitch roof trim pieces in place.

7. Use white light weight yarn to work Backstitches on roof and roof side trim.

8. Insert chimney in chimney opening of roof; tack in place with light yellow. Using photo as a guide, arrange flowers around chimney; glue or tack in place with white medium weight yarn.

Awning & Trellis

1. Cut all awning pieces from clear 7-count plastic canvas according to graphs (page 123).

2. Cut trellis pieces from white 7-count plastic canvas according to graph (page 122), cutting out four holes on each trellis.

3. Stitch awning pieces following graphs. Overcast bottom edges of awning trim pieces from white dot to white dot.

4. Using either the regular Whipstitch or a Binding Stitch throughout, stitch awning sides to awning where indicated between white dots. Stitch awning front trim and awning side trim pieces in place.

5. Using either the regular Overcast Stitch or a Binding Stitch, stitch remaining edges of awning.

6. Use white light weight yarn to work Backstitches and French Knots on awning.

7. Work embroidery on trellis pieces following graphs, combining lavender and purple light weight yarn for French Knots.

Shutters & Window Boxes

1. Cut shutters from clear 7-count plastic canvas, cut shutter flowers from 10-count plastic canvas according to graphs (page 122).

2. From clear 7-count plastic canvas, cut six 11-hole x 3-hole pieces for window box fronts and backs, six 2-hole x 3-hole pieces for window box ends and three 11-hole x 2-hole pieces for window box bases. Bases will remain unstitched.

3. Stitch window box front, back and ends with white Continental Stitches.

4. For each of the three window boxes, Whipstitch a front and a back to two ends. Whipstitch front, back and ends to a base. Overcast top edges.

5. Arrange and glue miniature artificial flowers in window boxes.

6. Following graphs throughout, stitch and Overcast shutters. Overcast shutter flowers.

7. Center one flower on each shutter and attach with lavender French Knot, working through both layers.

Birdhouse

1. Cut birdhouse front, back, base and roof pieces from 10-count plastic canvas according to graphs (page 123), cutting out hole in base.

2. Cut two 7-hole x 6-hole pieces for birdhouse sides from 10-count plastic canvas.

3. Paint dowel with white craft paint. Allow to dry.

4. Work birdhouse sides with white light weight yarn Continental Stitches. Stitch birdhouse front, back, base and roof pieces following graphs, working back entirely with white Continental Stitches.

5. Using either the regular Whipstitch, Overcast Stitch or a Binding Stitch through step 6, stitch front and back to sides. Stitch top edges. Do not Overcast inside edges on base.

6. Stitch roof pieces together along top edges. Stitch remaining edges.

7. Use white floss to work Backstitches on roof.

8. For perch, break off 1 inch (2.5cm) of toothpick. Insert about ½ inch (1.3cm) of pointed end into front where indicated on graph.

9. Insert one end of dowel approximately

1 inch (2.5cm) into hole on birdhouse base. Center roof over birdhouse. Glue in place.

Flowers & Signs

1. Cut 13 small flowers and four medium flowers from 10-count plastic canvas according to graphs (page 123).

2. Overcast six small flowers with lavender as graphed and seven with white. Work one lavender light weight French Knot in center of one white flower. Set aside.

3. Overcast four medium flowers with lavender. Work white floss French Knots; glue these flowers to trellis pieces where indicated with purple lines on graph, attaching bottom flower on left trellis to blue green "vine" over opening indicated.

4. Cut signs from 14-count plastic canvas according to graphs (page 123).

5. Stitch and Overcast signs following graphs,

Continued on page 120

Neon Bursts

Design by D.K. Designs

Skill Level

Beginner

Size

Fits boutique-style
tissue box

Materials

- 2½ sheets stiff 7-count
  plastic canvas
- Red Heart Super Saver Art.
  E300 medium weight yarn
  as listed in color key
- #16 tapestry needle

Instructions

1. Cut plastic canvas
according to graphs.
2. Stitch top and four sides
following graphs. Remaining
pieces will be used as liners
and will not be stitched.
3. Overcast inside edges
on top.
4. Place one liner behind
each side. Whipstitch sides
with liners together, working
through all four thicknesses.

Whipstitch sides and liners to top, working through all three thicknesses. Whipstitch bottom edges of sides and liners together. ■

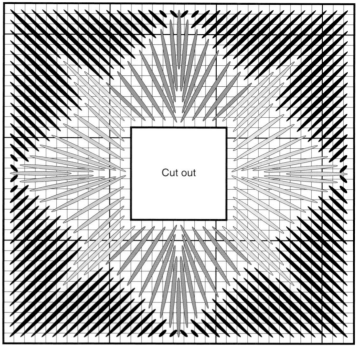

COLOR KEY

Yards	Medium Weight Yarn
4 (3.7m)	Pumpkin #254
26 (23.8m)	Black #312
3 (2.8m)	Bright yellow #324
4 (3.7m)	Turqua #512
4 (3.7m)	Spring green #672
4 (3.7m)	Shocking pink #718

Color numbers given are for Red Heart Super Saver Art. E300 medium weight yarn.

Top
33 holes x 33 holes
Cut 1

Side
33 holes x 37 holes
Cut 8, stitch 4

Shadow Diamonds

Design by D.K. Designs

Skill Level

Beginner

Size

Fits boutique-style
tissue box

Materials

- 2½ sheets stiff 7-count
  plastic canvas
- Uniek Needloft plastic
  canvas yarn as listed in
  color key
- Red Heart Super Saver
  Art. E300 medium
  weight yarn as listed
  in color key
- #16 tapestry needle

Instructions

1. Cut plastic canvas
according to graphs.
2. Stitch one top and four
sides following graphs.
Remaining pieces will be
used as liners and will not
be stitched.

3. Place liner behind top; Whipstitch inside edges together.

4. Place one liner behind each side. Whipstitch sides with liners together, working through all four thicknesses. Whipstitch sides and liners to top with liner, working through all four thicknesses. Whipstitch bottom edges of sides and liners together. ■

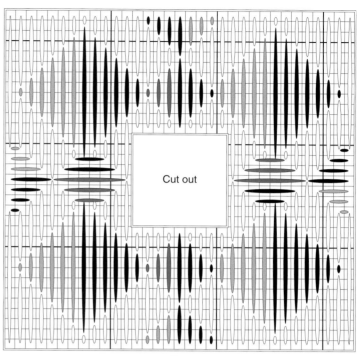

Top
33 holes x 33 holes
Cut 2, stitch 1

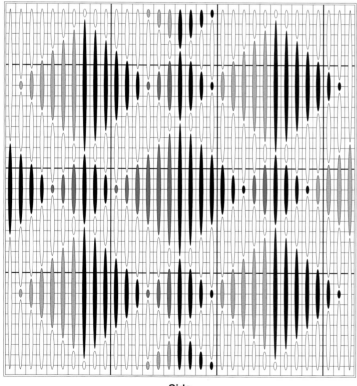

Side
33 holes x 36 holes
Cut 8, stitch 4

COLOR KEY

Yards	Plastic Canvas Yarn
15 (13.8m)	■ Black #00
6 (5.5m)	■ Red #01
28 (25.7m)	□ White #41
	Medium Weight Yarn
10 (9.2m)	■ Light gray #341

Color numbers given are for Uniek Needloft plastic canvas yarn and Red Heart Super Saver Art. E300 medium weight yarn.

God Bless You

Design by Alida Macor

Skill Level

Beginner

Size

Fits boutique-style tissue box

Materials

- 1½ sheets 7-count plastic canvas
- Medium weight yarn as listed in color key
- Darice metallic cord as listed in color key
- #16 tapestry needle
- 12 silver charms with a religious theme
- Hand-sewing needle
- White thread

Instructions

1. Cut plastic canvas according to graphs.

2. Stitch pieces following graphs. Overcast inside edges on top and bottom edges of sides.

3. Using hand-sewing needle and white thread, attach silver charms to sides where indicated on graph.

4. Whipstitch sides together, then Whipstitch sides to top. ■

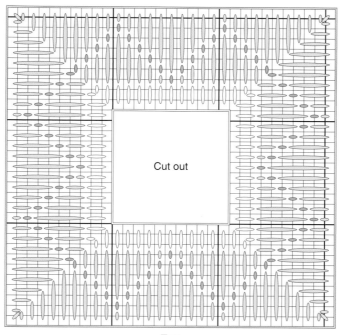

Top
31 holes x 31 holes
Cut 1

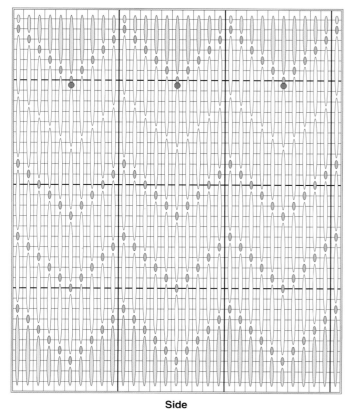

Side
31 holes x 37 holes
Cut 4

COLOR KEY		
Yards	**Medium Weight Yarn**	
30 (27.5m)	☐ White	
25 (22.9m)	☐ Baby blue	
	Metallic Cord	
10 (9.2m)	▨ Silver/white #3412-03	
	● Attach silver charm	

Color number given is for Darice metallic cord.

Spring Tulip Garden

Design by Alida Macor

Skill Level

Beginner

Size

Fits medium-count tissue box

Materials

- 1½ sheets 7-count plastic canvas
- Uniek Needloft plastic canvas yarn as listed in color key
- Medium weight yarn as listed in color key
- #16 tapestry needle

Instructions

1. Cut plastic canvas according to graphs (this page and page 125).

2. Stitch pieces following graphs. Overcast inside edges on top and bottom edges of sides and ends.

3. Whipstitch sides to ends, then Whipstitch sides and ends to top. ∎

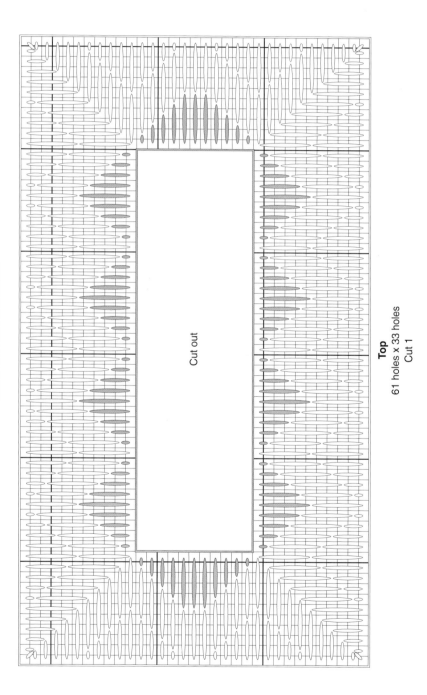

COLOR KEY

Yards	Plastic Canvas Yarn
2 (1.9m)	▨ Tangerine #11
20 (18.3m)	▨ Fern #23
4 (3.7m)	▨ Watermelon #55
2 (1.9m)	▨ Yellow #57
	Medium Weight Yarn
55 (50.3m)	☐ White

Color numbers given are for Uniek Needloft plastic canvas yarn.

Top
61 holes x 33 holes
Cut 1

Cut out

Graphs continued on page 125

Tropical Fish

Design by Terry Ricioli

Skill Level

Beginner

Size

Fits boutique-style
tissue box

Materials

- 1½ sheets 7-count
  plastic canvas
- Uniek Needloft plastic
  canvas yarn as listed
  in color key
- #16 tapestry needle

Instructions

1. Cut plastic canvas
according to graphs.
2. Stitch pieces following
graphs. Overcast inside
edges on top and bottom
edges of sides.
3. Whipstitch sides together,
then Whipstitch sides
to top. ■

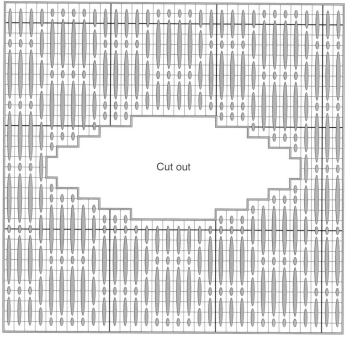

Top
32 holes x 32 holes
Cut 1

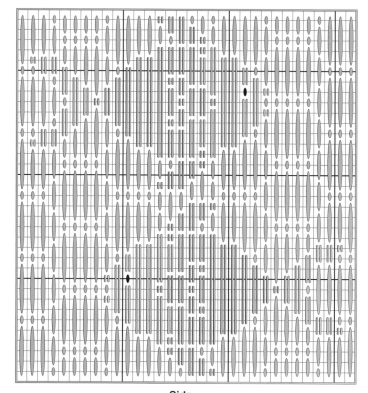

Side
32 holes x 36 holes
Cut 4

COLOR KEY	
Yards	**Plastic Canvas Yarn**
1 (1m)	■ Black #00
60 (54.9m)	▨ Bright blue #60
12 (11m)	⁄ Bright orange #58 Long Stitch
16 (14.7m)	⁄ Bright pink #62 Long Stitch
8 (7.4m)	⁄ Bright purple #64 Long Stitch
Color numbers given are for Uniek Needloft plastic canvas yarn.	

Continued from page 100

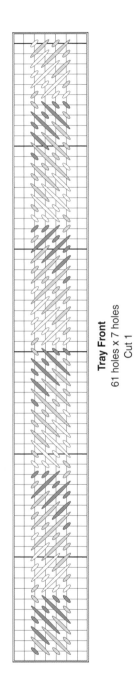

Tray Front
61 holes x 7 holes
Cut 1

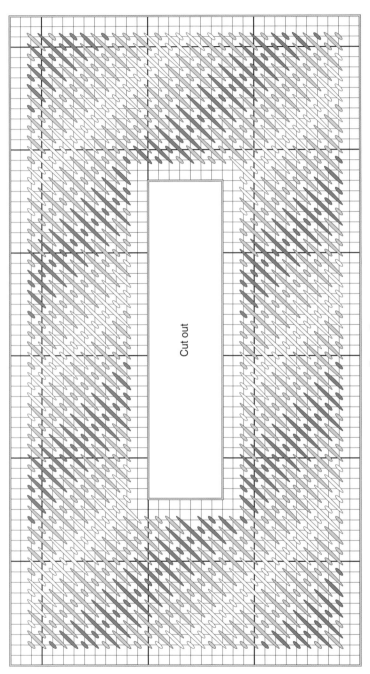

Cut out

Topper Top
63 holes x 33 holes
Cut 1

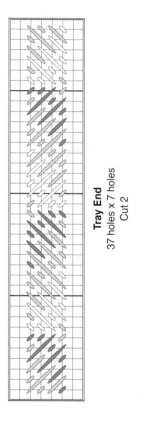

Tray End
37 holes x 7 holes
Cut 2

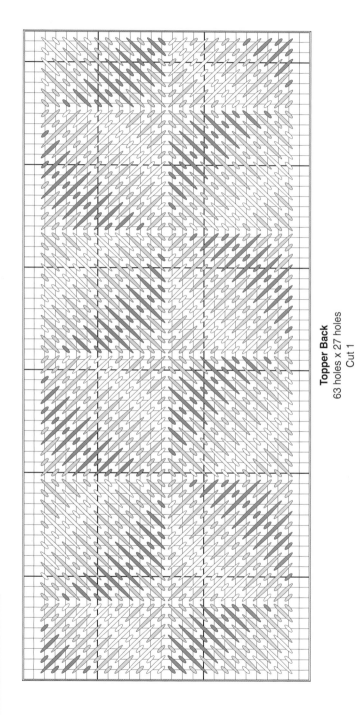

Topper Back
63 holes x 27 holes
Cut 1

COLOR KEY

Yards	Medium Weight Yarn
28 (25.7m)	☐ White #311
46 (42.1m)	■ Medium purple #528
66 (60.4m)	☐ Pale plum #579
	Uncoded areas are medium purple #528 Continental Stitches

Color numbers given are for Red Heart Super Saver Art. E300 medium weight yarn.

118 Vanity Tray

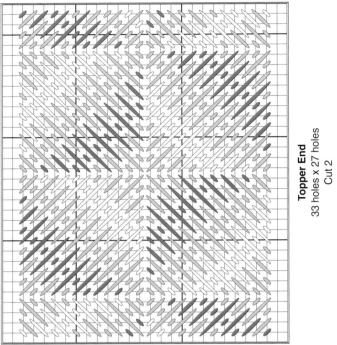

Topper End
33 holes x 27 holes
Cut 2

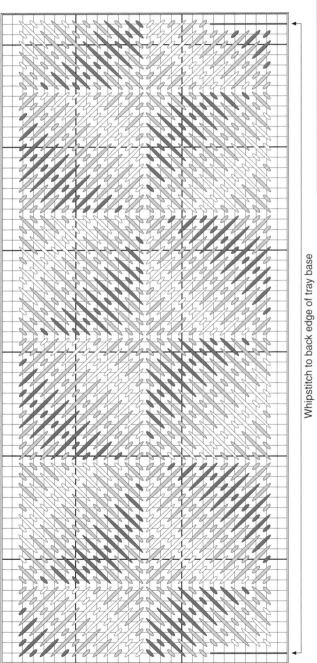

Whipstitch to back edge of tray base

Topper Front
63 holes x 27 holes
Cut 1

COLOR KEY	
Yards	**Medium Weight Yarn**
28 (25.7m)	☐ White #311
46 (42.1m)	■ Medium purple #528
66 (60.4m)	☐ Pale plum #579
	Uncoded areas are medium
	purple #528 Continental Stitches

Color numbers given are for Red Heart Super Saver
Art. E300 medium weight yarn.

Big Book of Tissue Toppers

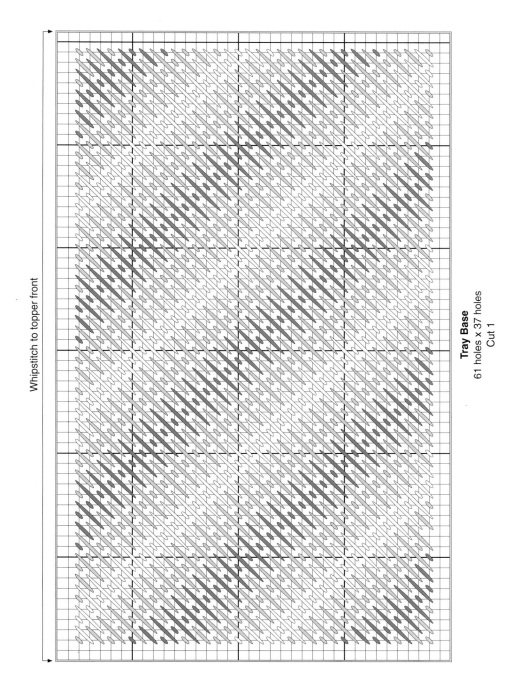

Whipstitch to topper front

Tray Base
61 holes x 37 holes
Cut 1

Flower Shop

Continued from page 105

working uncoded backgrounds with white floss Continental Stitches.

6. When background stitching and Overcasting are completed, embroider lettering.

Finishing

1. For flowers at bottom of shop back and sides, work purple French Knots to attach small purple flowers where indicated with purple lines and white flowers where indicated with red lines. Work remaining purple French Knots where indicated.

2. Center shop over opening on base; tack in place with light yellow and blue-green yarn.

3. Using photo as a guide throughout finishing, glue shutters in place on back and sides. Glue window boxes below back and side windows.

4. Using blue-green medium weight yarn throughout, tack top two rows of holes on trellises to bottom inside of awning sides. Center awning and trellises on front; tack bottom of trellises to base and awning to front.

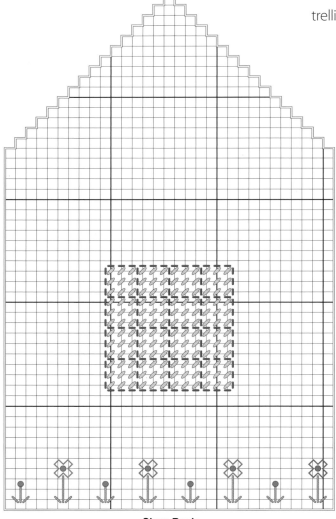

Shop Back
31 holes x 50 holes
Cut 1 from clear 7-count

COLOR KEY	
Yards	**Medium Weight Yarn**
150 (137.2m)	☐ Light yellow
150 (137.2m)	■ Blue-green
40 (36.6m)	☐ White
20 (18.3m)	☐ Pale gray
	Uncoded areas on shop front, back and sides are light yellow Continental Stitches
	⁄ Blue-green Backstitch and Straight Stitch
1 (1m)	◦ Bright yellow French Knot
	Light Weight Yarn
40 (36.6m)	■ White
5 (4.6m)	☐ Blue-green
20 (18.3m)	⁄ Lavender Overcast
	⁄ White Backstitch
	● White French Knot
	◦ Lavender French Knot
10 (9.2m)	● Purple French Knot
	◦ Lavender and purple (combined) French Knot
	6-Strand Embroidery Floss
10 (9.2m)	Uncoded backgrounds on signs are white Continental Stitches
4 (3.7m)	⁄ Blue-green Overcast
	⁄ White Backstitch and Overcast
3 (2.8m)	⁄ Dark green Backstitch, Straight Stitch and Overcast
3 (2.8m)	⁄ Black Backstitch
1 (1m)	⁄ Light green Backstitch and Straight Stitch
	● White French Knot
	Cloisonné Metallic Thread
1 (1m)	◦ Gold French Knot
	● Attach toothpick perch
	✹ Attach small purple flower
	✹ Attach small white flower

5. Use blue-green floss to tack "Open" sign to left side of door and shop sign above awning.

6. Center and glue shop roof in place.

7. Position birdhouse at front left corner of shop, gluing edge of roof to corner of shop and bottom of dowel into base. Glue remaining small white flower to bottom of dowel and to base.

8. Glue trims and embellishments as desired to shop and base. ■

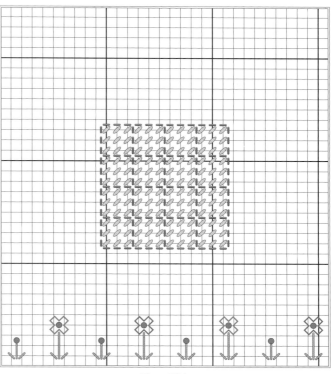

Shop Side
31 holes x 35 holes
Cut 2 from clear 7-count

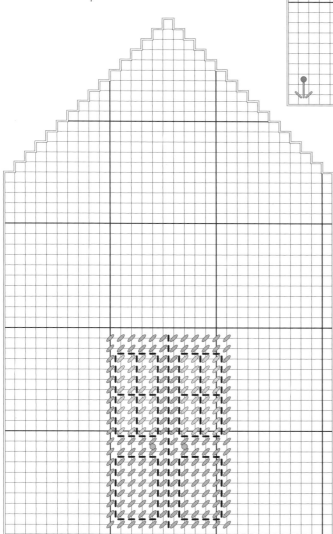

Shop Front
31 holes x 50 holes
Cut 1 from clear 7-count

Chimney Flower
5 holes x 5 holes
Cut 4 from clear 7-count

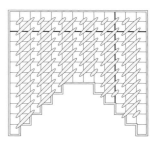

Chimney Front & Back
13 holes x 12 holes
Cut 2 from clear 7-count

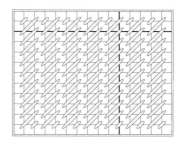

Chimney Side
15 holes x 12 holes
Cut 2 from clear 7-count

Shutter
5 holes x 12 holes
Cut 6 from clear 7-count

Shutter Flower
5 holes x 5 holes
Cut 6 from 10-count

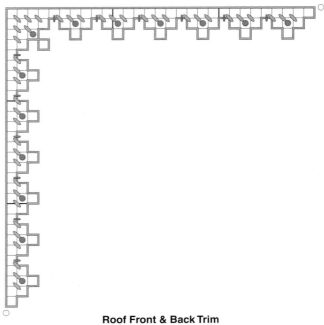

Roof Front & Back Trim
29 holes x 29 holes
Cut 2 from clear 7-count

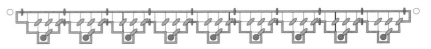

Roof Side Trim
37 holes x 3 holes
Cut 2 from clear 7-count

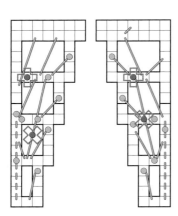

Trellises
7 holes x 18 holes each
Cut 1 each from white 7-count

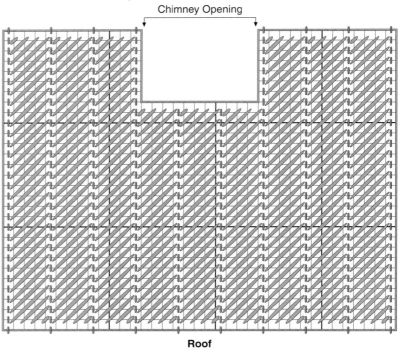

Chimney Opening

Roof
37 holes x 29 holes
Cut 2 from clear 7-count

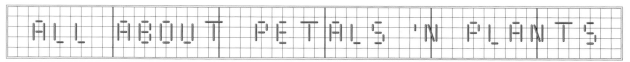

Shop Sign
58 holes x 5 holes
Cut 1 from 14-count

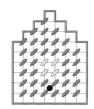

Birdhouse Front & Back
7 holes x 9 holes
Cut 2 from 10-count
Stitch front as graphed
Stitch back entirely with
white Continental Stitches

Birdhouse Base
7 holes x 7 holes
Cut 1 from 10-count

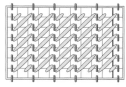

Birdhouse Roof
11 holes x 7 holes
Cut 2 from 10-count

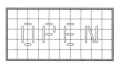

"Open" Sign
10 holes x 5 holes
Cut 1 from 14-count

Small Flower
3 holes x 3 holes
Cut 13 from 10-count
Overcast 6 as graphed
Overcast 7 with white

Medium Flower
3 holes x 3 holes
Cut 4 from 10-count

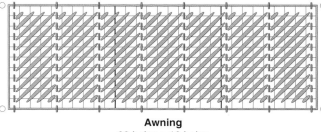

Awning
29 holes x 10 holes
Cut 1 from clear 7-count

Awning Front Trim
29 holes x 3 holes
Cut 1 from clear 7-count

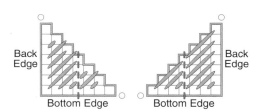

Awning Sides
7 holes x 7 holes each
Cut 1 each from clear 7-count

Awning Side Trim
7 holes x 3 holes
Cut 2 from clear 7-count

COLOR KEY

Yards	Medium Weight Yarn
150 (137.2m)	□ Light yellow
150 (137.2m)	▨ Blue-green
40 (36.6m)	□ White
20 (18.3m)	▨ Pale gray
	Uncoded areas on shop front, back and sides are light yellow Continental Stitches
	╱ Blue-green Backstitch and Straight Stitch
1 (1m)	● Bright yellow French Knot

Light Weight Yarn

40 (36.6m)	▨ White
5 (4.6m)	□ Blue-green
20 (18.3m)	╱ Lavender Overcast
	╱ White Backstitch
	● White French Knot
	○ Lavender French Knot
10 (9.2m)	● Purple French Knot
	● Lavender and purple (combined) French Knot

6-Strand Embroidery Floss

10 (9.2m)	Uncoded backgrounds on signs are white Continental Stitches
4 (3.7m)	╱ Blue-green Overcast
	╱ White Backstitch and Overcast
3 (2.8m)	╱ Dark green Backstitch, Straight Stitch and Overcast
3 (2.8m)	╱ Black Backstitch
1 (1m)	╱ Light green Backstitch and Straight Stitch
	● White French Knot

Cloisonné Metallic Thread

1 (1m)	● Gold French Knot
	● Attach toothpick perch
	✖ Attach small purple flower
	✖ Attach small white flower

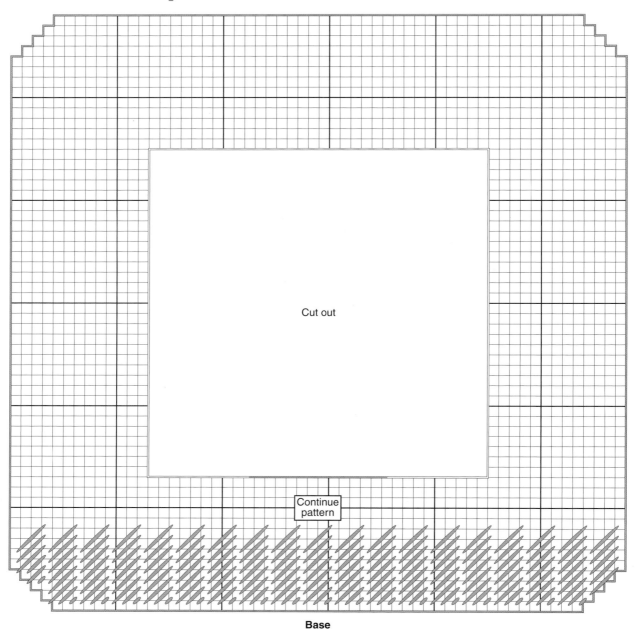

Base
58 holes x 58 holes
Cut 1 from clear 7-count

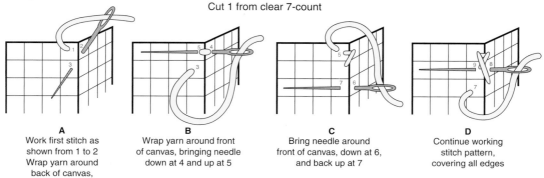

A
Work first stitch as
shown from 1 to 2
Wrap yarn around
back of canvas,
bringing needle up at 3

B
Wrap yarn around front
of canvas, bringing needle
down at 4 and up at 5

C
Bring needle around
front of canvas, down at 6,
and back up at 7

D
Continue working
stitch pattern,
covering all edges

Binding Stitch

Continued from page 113

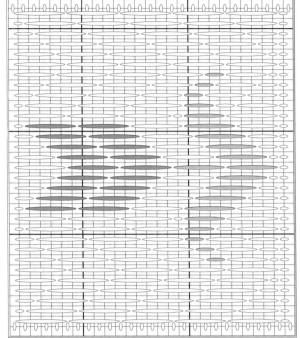

End
33 holes x 27 holes
Cut 2

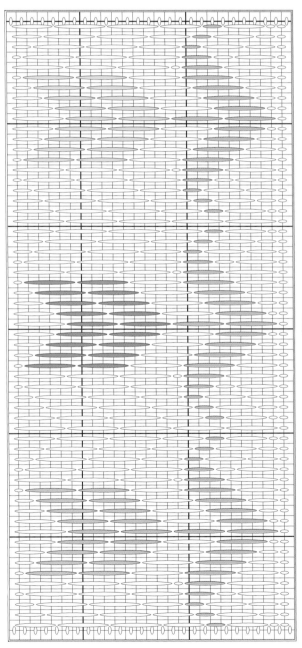

Side
61 holes x 27 holes
Cut 2

COLOR KEY	
Yards	**Plastic Canvas Yarn**
2 (1.9m)	Tangerine #11
20 (18.3m)	Fern #23
4 (3.7m)	Watermelon #55
2 (1.9m)	Yellow #57
	Medium Weight Yarn
55 (50.3m)	White

Color numbers given are for Uniek
Needloft plastic canvas yarn.

Quilt Look

Dazzling Dahlia

Design by Debra Arch

Skill Level

Beginner

Size

Fits boutique-style tissue box

Materials

- 1½ sheets 7-count plastic canvas
- Red Heart Super Saver Art. E300 medium weight yarn as listed in color key
- #16 tapestry needle

Instructions

1. Cut plastic canvas according to graphs.

2. Stitch pieces following graphs, working two spring green Straight Stitches per hole where indicated as part of the background stitching and working uncoded areas with white Continental Stitches.

3. When background stitching is completed, work black Straight Stitches.

4. Overcast inside edges on top, and bottom edges of sides. Whipstitch sides together, then Whipstitch sides to top. ■

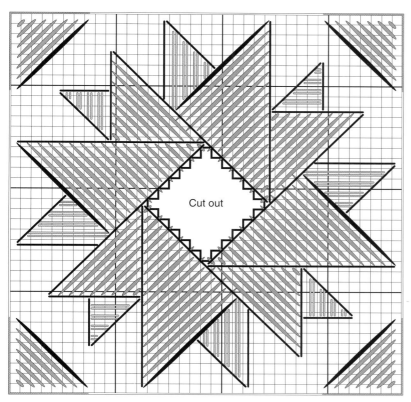

Top
37 holes x 37 holes
Cut 1

COLOR KEY

Yards	Medium Weight Yarn
58 (53.1m)	☐ White #311
18 (16.5m)	■ Black #312
54 (49.4m)	▨ Medium purple #528
30 (27.5m)	▨ Spring green #672

Uncoded areas are
white Continental Stitches
✦ Black #312 Straight Stitch
✦ Spring green #672
Straight Stitch
Color numbers given are for Red Heart Super
Saver Art. E300 medium weight yarn.

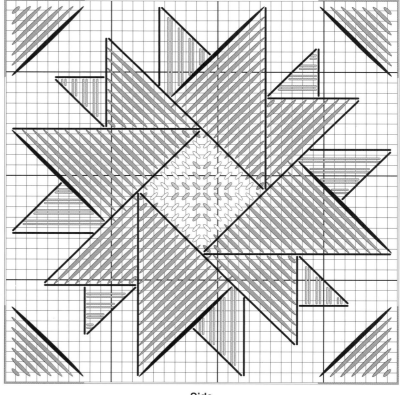

Side
37 holes x 37 holes
Cut 4

Southwest Star & Arrow

Design by Angie Arickx

Skill Level

Beginner

Size

Fits boutique-style tissue box

Materials

- 2 sheets 7-count plastic canvas
- Red Heart Classic Art. E267 medium weight yarn as listed in color key
- Red Heart Super Saver Art. E300 medium weight yarn as listed in color key
- #16 tapestry needle

Instructions

1. Cut plastic canvas according to graphs.

2. Stitch pieces following graphs, working two Aran and linen Straight Stitches per hole where indicated as part of the background stitching.

3. Overcast inside edges on top, and bottom edges of sides. Whipstitch sides together, then Whipstitch sides to top. ■

Top
31 holes x 31 holes
Cut 1

Side
31 holes x 37 holes
Cut 4

COLOR KEY	
Yards	**Medium Weight Yarn**
12 (11m)	■ Teal #48
22 (20.2m)	■ Bronze #286
15 (13.8m)	■ Copper #289
14 (12.9m)	■ Dusty teal #657
22 (20.2m)	✎ Aran #313 Straight Stitch, Overcast and Whipstitch
12 (11m)	✎ Linen #330 Straight Stitch
Color numbers given are for Red Heart Classic Art. E267 and Super Saver Art. E300 medium weight yarn.	

Autumn Leaves

Design by D.K. Designs

Skill Level

Beginner

Size

Fits boutique-style tissue box

Materials

- 2½ sheets stiff 7-count plastic canvas
- Red Heart Super Saver Art. E300 medium weight yarn as listed in color key
- #16 tapestry needle

Instructions

1. Cut plastic canvas according to graphs (page 143).

2. Stitch one top and four sides following graphs. Remaining pieces will be used as liners and will not be stitched.

3. Place liner behind top; Whipstitch inside edges together.

4. Place one liner behind each side. Whipstitch sides with liners together, working through all four layers. Whipstitch sides and liners to top with liner, working through all four layers. Whipstitch bottom edges of sides and liners together. ■

Graphs on page 143

Swamp Angels

Design by Alida Macor

Skill Level

Beginner

Size

Fits boutique-style tissue box

Materials

- 1½ sheets 7-count plastic canvas
- Medium weight yarn as listed in color key
- #16 tapestry needle
- 16 (5mm) white pearl beads
- Hand-sewing needle
- White thread

Instructions

1. Cut plastic canvas according to graphs.

2. Stitch pieces following graphs.

3. When background stitching is completed, use hand-sewing needle and white thread to attach beads to sides where indicated on graph.

4. Overcast inside edges on top, and bottom edges of sides. Whipstitch sides together, then Whipstitch sides to top. ■

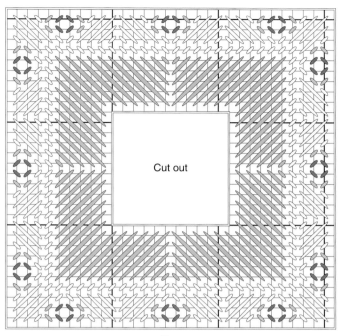

Top
31 holes x 31 holes
Cut 1

Side
31 holes x 37 holes
Cut 4

COLOR KEY

Yards	Medium Weight Yarn
40 (36.6m)	☐ White
25 (22.9m)	■ Purple
21 (19.3m)	☐ Lavender
17 (15.6m)	☐ Medium green
	○ Attach bead

Garden Path

Design by Gina Woods

Skill Level

Intermediate

Size

Fits boutique-style tissue box

Materials

- 1½ sheets 7-count plastic canvas
- Medium weight yarn as listed in color key
- #16 tapestry needle

Instructions

1. Cut plastic canvas according to graphs.

2. Stitch sides A following graph, working uncoded areas on white background with black Continental Stitches and uncoded areas on yellow background with black Reverse Continental Stitches.

3. Stitch sides B, following instructions in step 2 and switching colors on flowers as follows: lavender and medium coral, orchid and light coral.

4. When background stitching is completed, work lime green Backstitches and Straight Stitches.

5. Overcast inside edges on top, and bottom edges of sides. Whipstitch sides A to sides B, making sure sides with matching flowers are opposite each other. Whipstitch sides to top. ■

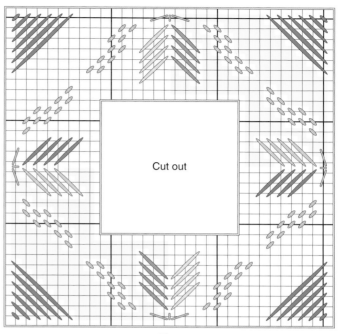

Top
31 holes x 31 holes
Cut 1

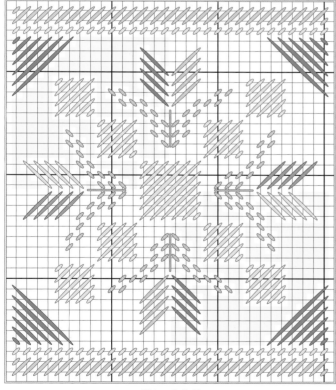

Sides A & B
31 holes x 37 holes
Cut 4
Stitch 2 sides A as graphed
Stitch 2 sides B, switching
lavender and medium coral,
and orchid and light coral
on flowers only

COLOR KEY
Yards	Medium Weight Yarn
28 (25.7m)	☐ Aqua
10 (9.2m)	☐ Orchid
10 (9.2m)	☐ Lime
6 (5.5m)	☐ Medium blue
3 (2.8m)	☐ Medium coral
3 (2.8m)	☐ Light coral
3 (2.8m)	☐ Lavender
40 (36.6m)	Uncoded areas on white background are black Continental Stitches
	Uncoded areas on yellow background are black Reverse Continental Stitches
	╱ Lime Backstitch and Straight Stitch

Goose in the Pond

Design by Gina Woods

Skill Level

Beginner

Size

Fits boutique-style tissue box

Materials

- 1½ sheets 7-count plastic canvas
- Medium weight yarn as listed in color key
- #16 tapestry needle

Instructions

1. Cut plastic canvas according to graphs.

2. Stitch pieces following graphs, working uncoded areas on white background with white Continental Stitches and uncoded areas on blue background with teal Continental Stitches.

3. Overcast inside edges on top, and bottom edges of sides. Whipstitch sides together, then Whipstitch sides to top. ■

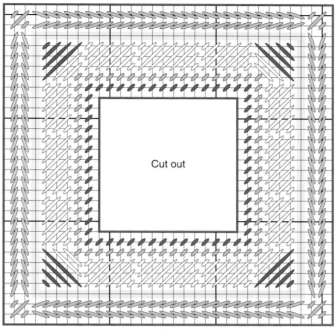

Top
31 holes x 31 holes
Cut 1

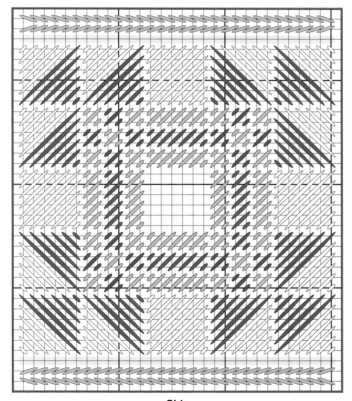

Side
31 holes x 37 holes
Cut 4

COLOR KEY	
Yards	**Medium Weight Yarn**
40 (36.6m)	☐ White
32 (29.3m)	▨ Light plum
22 (20.2m)	■ Teal
12 (11m)	■ Dark plum
6 (5.5m)	▨ Lime
4 (3.7m)	■ Forest green

Uncoded areas on white
background are white
Continental Stitches
Uncoded areas on blue
background are teal
Continental Stitches

Sunflower Pinwheel

Design by Angie Arickx

Skill Level

Beginner

Size

Fits family-size tissue box

Materials

- 2 sheets 7-count plastic canvas
- Uniek Needloft plastic canvas yarn as listed in color key
- #16 tapestry needle

Instructions

1. Cut plastic canvas according to graphs (pages 141 and 142).

2. Stitch pieces following graphs, working uncoded areas with fern Continental Stitches.

3. Overcast inside edges on top, and bottom edges of sides and ends. Whipstitch sides to ends, then Whipstitch sides and ends to top. ∎

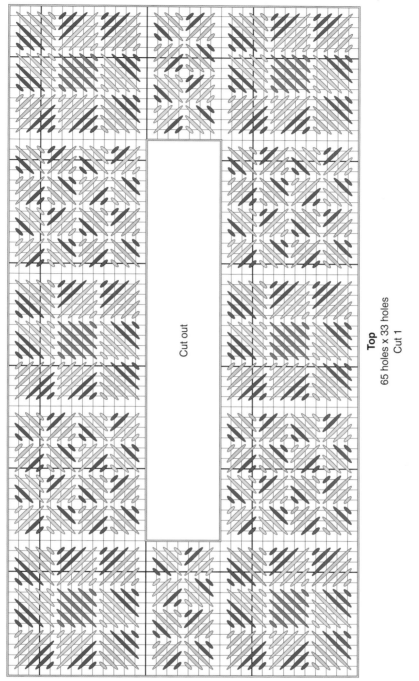

Cut out

Top
65 holes x 33 holes
Cut 1

COLOR KEY

Yards	Plastic Canvas Yarn
25 (22.9m)	☐ Tangerine #11
8 (7.4m)	■ Brown #15
30 (27.5m)	■ Holly #27
25 (22.9m)	☐ Yellow #57
20 (18.3m)	Uncoded areas are fern #23 Continental Stitches
	╱ Fern #23 Overcast and Whipstitch

Color numbers given are for Uniek Needloft plastic canvas yarn.

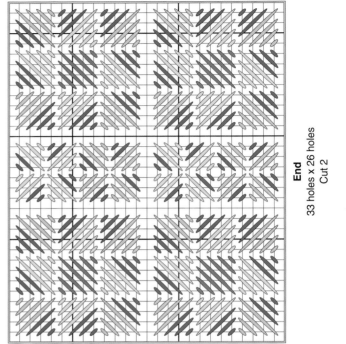

End
33 holes x 26 holes
Cut 2

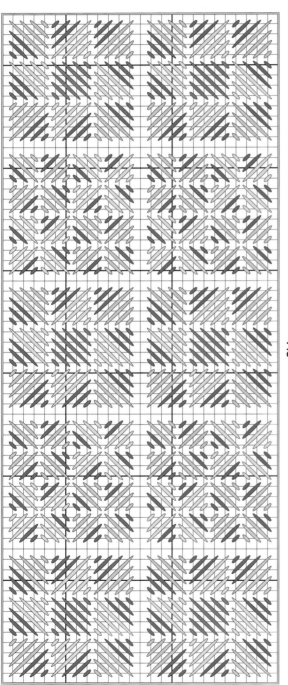

Side
65 holes x 26 holes
Cut 2

COLOR KEY	
Yards	**Plastic Canvas Yarn**
25 (22.9m)	Tangerine #11
8 (7.4m)	Brown #15
30 (27.5m)	Holly #27
25 (22.9m)	Yellow #57
20 (18.3m)	Uncoded areas are fern #23 Continental Stitches
	Fern #23 Overcast and Whipstitch

Color numbers given are for Uniek Needloft plastic canvas yarn.

Autumn Leaves

Continued from page 132

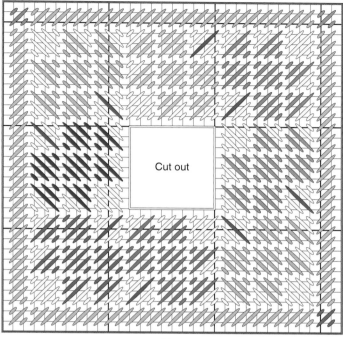

Top
32 holes x 32 holes
Cut 2, stitch 1

Side
32 holes x 36 holes
Cut 8, stitch 4

COLOR KEY	
Yards	**Medium Weight Yarn**
5 (4.6m)	☐ Carrot #256
9 (8.3m)	☐ Aran #313
6 (5.5m)	☐ Gold #321
3 (2.8m)	☐ Ranch red #332
13 (11.9m)	☐ Warm brown #336
4 (3.7m)	☐ Coffee #365
3 (2.8m)	☐ Burgundy #376
3 (2.8m)	☐ Claret #378
3 (2.8m)	☐ Light sage #631
6 (5.5m)	☐ Dark sage #633

Color numbers given are for Red Heart Super Saver Art. E300 medium weight yarn.

Potpourri

Starfish

Design by Terry Ricioli

Skill Level

Beginner

Size

Fits boutique-style tissue box

Materials

- 1½ sheets 7-count plastic canvas
- 4 (5-inch) Uniek QuickShape plastic canvas stars
- Uniek Needloft plastic canvas yarn as listed in color key
- #16 tapestry needle
- Hot-glue gun

Instructions

1. Cut plastic canvas according to graphs, cutting away gray area on stars (starfish).

2. Following graphs throughout all stitching, stitch and Overcast starfish. Work camel and pale peach Straight Stitches when background stitching is completed.

3. Stitch topper pieces, working uncoded areas with sail blue Continental Stitches.

4. Overcast inside edges on top and bottom edges of sides. Whipstitch sides together, then Whipstitch sides to top.

5. Center and glue starfish to sides. ■

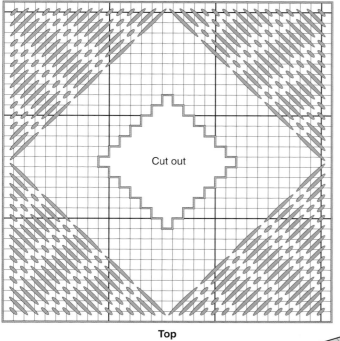

Top
31 holes x 31 holes
Cut 1

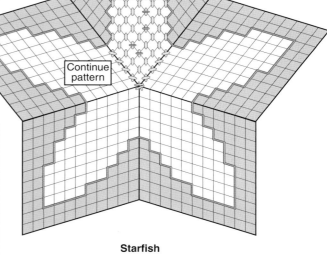

Starfish
Cut 4 from plastic canvas stars,
cutting away gray area

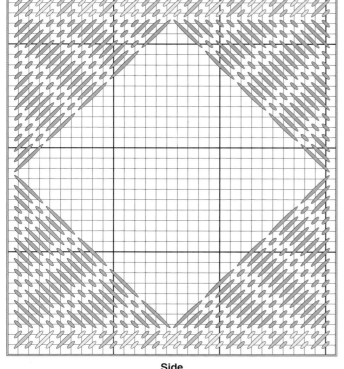

Side
31 holes x 35 holes
Cut 4

COLOR KEY

Yards	Plastic Canvas Yarn
42 (38.4m)	☐ Sail blue #35
48 (43.9m)	☐ Camel #43
28 (25.7m)	☐ Pale peach #56

Uncoded areas are sail blue
#35 Continental Stitches
✎ Camel #43 Straight Stitch
✎ Pale peach #56 Straight Stitch
Color numbers given are for Uniek Needloft plastic
canvas yarn.

Pool Shark

Design by Mary T. Cosgrove

Skill Level

Beginner

Size

Fits boutique-style tissue box

Materials

- 1½ sheets 7-count plastic canvas
- Uniek Needloft plastic canvas yarn as listed in color key
- #16 tapestry needle

Instructions

1. Cut plastic canvas according to graphs.

2. Stitch pieces following graphs, working uncoded areas with Christmas green Continental Stitches.

3. When background stitching is completed, work Christmas green Backstitches on sides A and black Backstitches on sides B.

4. Overcast inside edges on top and bottom edges of sides. Whipstitch sides A to sides B, then Whipstitch sides to top. ∎

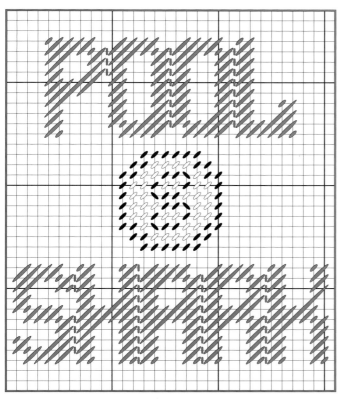

Side A
31 holes x 37 holes
Cut 2

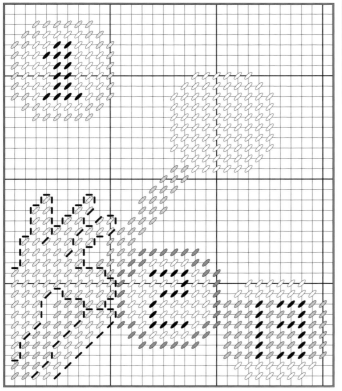

Side B
31 holes x 37 holes
Cut 2

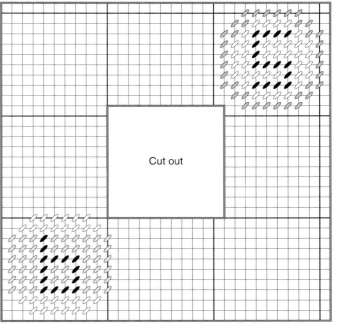

Cut out

Top
31 holes x 31 holes
Cut 1

COLOR KEY

Yards	Plastic Canvas Yarn
9 (8.3m)	■ Black #00
12 (11m)	■ Red #01
4 (3.7m)	☐ Pink #07
2 (1.9m)	■ Royal #32
12 (11m)	☐ White #41
2 (1.9m)	☐ Camel #43
3 (2.8m)	☐ Yellow #57
3 (2.8m)	■ Bright orange #58
56 (51.3m)	Uncoded areas are Christmas green #28 Continental Stitches
	╱ Christmas green #28 Backstitch, Overcast and Whipstitch
	╱ Black #00 Backstitch

Color numbers given are for Uniek Needloft plastic canvas yarn.

Hot-Pink Purse

Design by Debra Arch

Skill Level

Intermediate

Size

Fits boutique-style tissue box, approximately 8¼ inches W x 10⅞ inches H (21cm x 27.6cm)

Materials

- 1½ sheets 7-count plastic canvas
- 2 (9-inch) Uniek QuickShape plastic canvas radial circles
- Lion Brand Fun Fur Article #320 bulky weight eyelash yarn as listed in color key
- Kreinik ⅛-inch Ribbon as listed in color key
- #16 tapestry needle
- 2-inch (5.1cm) silver embellishment or jewelry pin (sample used silver beaded star)
- Clean toothbrush
- Hot-glue gun

Project Note

Use 2 strands hot pink yarn and silver ribbon for all stitching.

Instructions

1. Cut plastic canvas according to graphs (this page and pages 152 and 170), cutting away gray area on circles (handle).

2. Stitch pieces following graphs, reversing one handle before stitching.

3. Overcast inside edges on top and bottom edges of sides. Whipstitch sides together, then Whipstitch sides to top, easing as necessary to fit. Whipstitch wrong sides of handles together.

4. Using photo as a guide throughout, glue handle ends to purse sides. Glue silver embellishment or pin to front of purse. ■

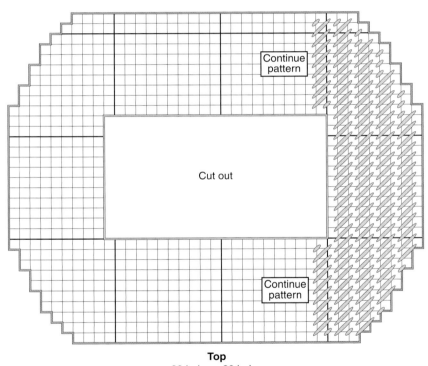

Top
39 holes x 32 holes
Cut 1

COLOR KEY	
Yards	**Bulky Weight Eyelash Yarn**
128 (117.1m)	▨ Hot pink #195 (2 strands)
	¹/₈-Inch Ribbon
15 (13.8m)	☐ Silver #001 (2 strands)

Color numbers given are for Lion Brand Fun Fur Article #320 bulky weight eyelash yarn and Kreinik ¹/₈-inch Ribbon.

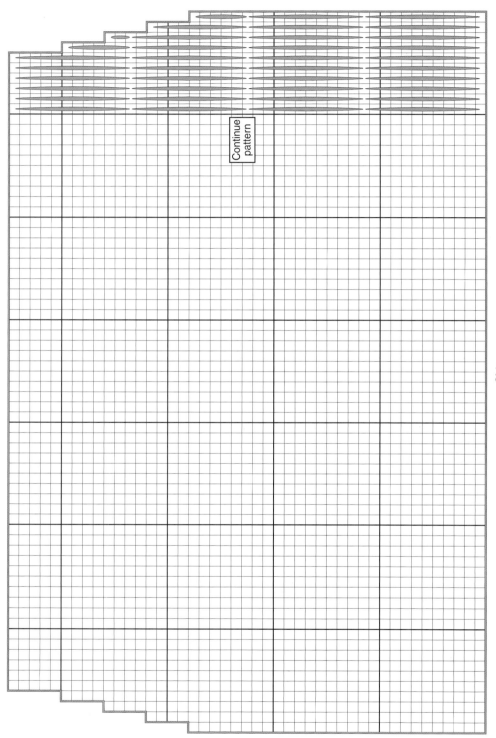

Side
70 holes x 45 holes
Cut 2

Continue pattern

Graphs continued on page 170

Pink Ribbon

Design by Nancy Dorman

Skill Level

Beginner

Size

Fits boutique-style tissue box

Materials

- 2 sheets 7-count plastic canvas
- Medium weight yarn as listed in color key
- 6-strand embroidery floss as listed in color key
- #16 tapestry needle

Instructions

1. Cut plastic canvas according to graphs (page 171).

2. Stitch and Overcast pink ribbons following graph. For each ribbon, fold one end over the other to form loop; tack in center with pink yarn.

3. Stitch topper pieces following graphs. When background stitching is completed, work rose Backstitches and French Knots.

4. Using regular Overcast Stitch and Whipstitch or a Binding Stitch (page 171), stitch inside edges on top and bottom edges of sides. Stitch sides together, then stitch sides to top.

5. Center one ribbon on each side and tack in place with pink yarn. ∎

Graphs on page 171

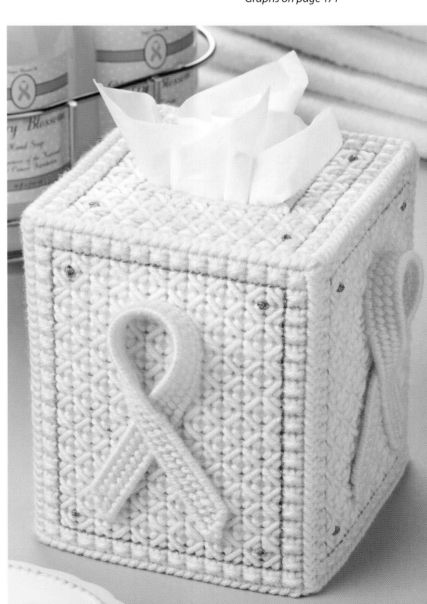

Nautical

Design by Deborah Scheblein

Skill Level

Beginner

Size

Fits boutique-style tissue box

Materials

- 2 sheets 7-count plastic canvas
- Medium weight yarn as listed in color key
- #16 tapestry needle
- 2 (18-inch/45.7cm) lengths narrow white cord
- Hot-glue gun

Instructions

1. Cut plastic canvas according to graphs (pages 155 and 172), cutting out one hole each in top, anchor and life preserver, and cutting out eight holes in wheel.

2. Stitch topper pieces following graphs, working uncoded areas with dark country blue Continental Stitches and working light blue Straight Stitches

as part of the background stitching.

3. Stitch and Overcast remaining pieces, working brown and cream Straight Stitches on sailboat when background stitching is completed.

4. Overcast inside edges on top and bottom edges of sides. Whipstitch sides together, then Whipstitch sides to top.

5. Tie an end of one length of cord through opening at top of anchor. Center anchor on one side. Loop and entwine cord as desired from top down to and around one arm and fluke of anchor. Glue anchor and cord in place. Trim any excess cord.

6. Weave remaining cord under stitching on back side of life preserver where indicated with green lines, allowing ⅜–⅝-inch (1–1.6cm) loops to extend beyond edges of white areas. Trim excess cord. Center and glue life preserver to one side.

7. Center and glue wheel and sailboat to remaining sides. ∎

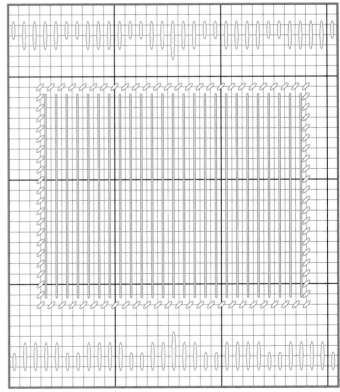

COLOR KEY

Yards	Medium Weight Yarn
15 (13.8m)	□ Cream
6 (5.5m)	■ Brown
4 (3.7m)	□ White
3 (2.8m)	■ Red
37 (33.9m)	Uncoded areas are dark country blue Continental Stitches
	⁄ Dark country blue Overcast and Whipstitch
2 (1.9m)	⁄ Dark tan Overcast
16 (14.7m)	⁄ Light blue Straight Stitch
	⁄ Cream Straight Stitch
	⁄ Brown Straight Stitch

Side
31 holes x 37 holes
Cut 4

Graphs continued on page 172

Country Clothesline

Design by Deborah Scheblein

Skill Level

Beginner

Size

Fits boutique-style tissue box

Materials

- 2 sheets 7-count plastic canvas
- Medium weight yarn as listed in color key
- 6-strand embroidery floss as listed in color key
- #16 tapestry needle
- 16 mini clothespins
- 24 inches (61cm) string
- Hot-glue gun

Instructions

1. Cut plastic canvas according to graphs (pages 158, 159 and 173).

2. Stitch topper pieces following graphs, working Continental Stitches in uncoded areas as follows: white background with light blue, green background with green.

3. When background stitching is completed, randomly work yellow French Knots for dandelions in grass on back and sides, leaving an area clear on one side for laundry basket. Do not add French Knots inside red lines on back.

4. Stitch and Overcast remaining pieces, working one small towel with lavender as graphed and one with magenta; work two socks as graphed and two socks entirely with white.

5. When background stitching and Overcasting are completed, work black embroidery on birdhouse, white yarn embroidery on towels, and white floss embroidery on blue jeans.

6. Overcast inside edges on top and bottom edges of sides and back. Whipstitch sides and back together, then Whipstitch sides to top.

7. Thread string (clothesline) from back to front through one clothesline pole where indicated on graph, anchoring end on back side. Glue pole to back where indicated on graph with red lines.

8. Wrap string around topper. Thread string from front to back through remaining clothesline pole where indicated, anchoring end on back side; trim excess string. **Note:** *Make sure clothesline does not sag.* Glue pole to other side of back where indicated with red lines.

9. Attach laundry to clothesline with mini clothespins; glue in place. Glue laundry basket in place. ∎

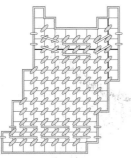

Large Towel
11 holes x 14 holes
Cut 1

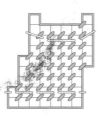

Small Towel
8 holes x 9 holes
Cut 2
Stitch 1 as graphed
Stitch 1 replacing
lavender with magenta

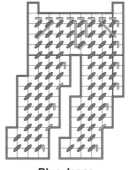

Blue Jeans
11 holes x 15 holes
Cut 1

Sock
4 holes x 7 holes
Cut 4
Stitch 2 as graphed
Stitch 2 entirely
with white

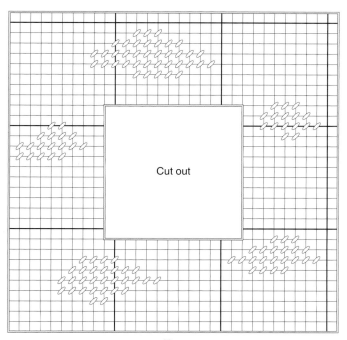

Top
31 holes x 31 holes
Cut 1

COLOR KEY

Yards	Medium Weight Yarn
11 (10.1m)	☐ White
10 (9.2m)	■ Forest
5 (4.6m)	☐ Tan
3 (2.8m)	■ Red
3 (2.8m)	■ Dark country blue
3 (2.8m)	■ Bright pink
2 (1.9m)	☐ Salmon
2 (1.9m)	☐ Medium clay
1 (1m)	☐ Lavender
1 (1m)	■ Dark brown
1 (1m)	Magenta
45 (41.2m)	Uncoded areas on white background are light blue Continental Stitches
27 (24.7m)	Uncoded areas on green background are green Continental Stitches
	╱ Light blue Overcast and Whipstitch
	╱ Green Overcast and Whipstitch
	╱ White Backstitch
1 (1m)	╱ Black Backstitch
2 (1.9m)	Yellow French Knot
	6-Strand Embroidery Floss
1 (1m)	╱ White Backstitch, Straight Stitch and Running Stitch
	● Attach string

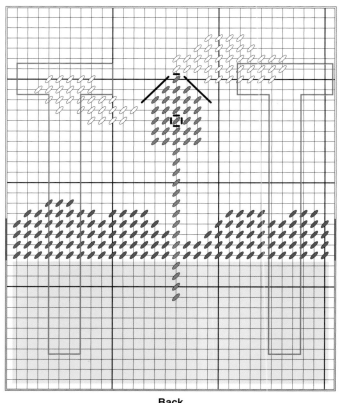

Back
31 holes x 37 holes
Cut 1

Graphs continued on page 173

Music Lovers

Design by Mildred Goeppel

Skill Level

Beginner

Size

Fits boutique-style tissue box

Materials

- 1½ sheets 7-count plastic canvas
- Medium weight yarn as listed in color key
- #16 tapestry needle

Instructions

1. Cut plastic canvas according to graphs. ***Note:*** *Sides A are one hole narrower than sides B.*

2. Stitch pieces following graphs, working black stitches first on sides A and B.

3. Overcast inside edges on top and bottom edges of sides. Whipstitch sides A to sides B, making sure to place sides A opposite each other, and sides B opposite each other. Whipstitch sides to top. ■

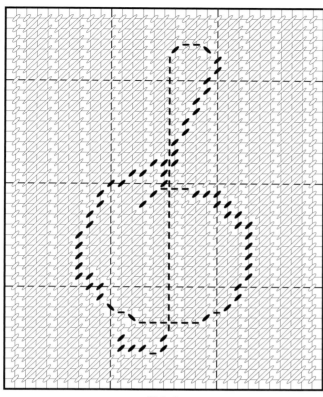

Side A
30 holes x 37 holes
Cut 2

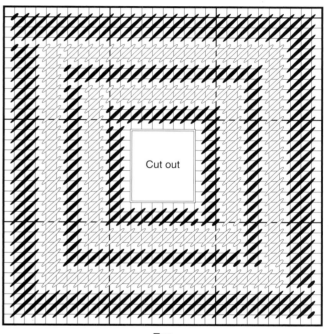

Top
30 holes x 31 holes
Cut 1

Cut out

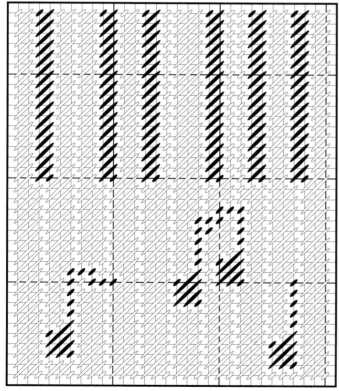

Side B
31 holes x 37 holes
Cut 2

COLOR KEY		
Yards	**Medium Weight Yarn**	
42 (38.4m)	☐ White	
24 (22m)	■ Black	
	✦ Black Backstitch and Straight Stitch	

Alligator

Design by Joanne Wetzel

Skill Level

Advanced

Size

Fits regular-size tissue box
Alligator is approximately 11¼ inches W x
20¼ inches L x 3⅞ inches H (28.6cm x
51.4cm x 9.8cm)

Materials

- 7 sheets 7-count plastic canvas
- Medium weight yarn as listed in color key
- #16 tapestry needle
- 2 (15mm) yellow cat eyes with washer
- Hot-glue gun

Project Note

Right and left are designated according to
alligator's point of view. Left side is alligator's
actual left side and right side is alligator's
actual right side.

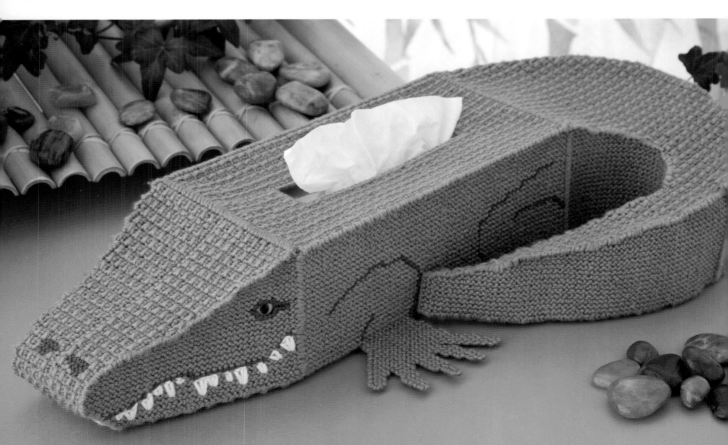

Instructions

1. Cut plastic canvas according to graphs (pages 164–169), cutting out hole in top and head sides.

2. Cut two 34-hole x 24-hole pieces for cover ends and two 5-hole x 5-hole pieces for eye holders. Ends will remain unstitched.

3. Using white, stitch eye holders with Continental Stitches. Do not overcast edges.

4. Following graphs throughout all stitching, work medium olive green and white stitches first on head sides; fill in remaining areas with light olive green stitches, completely covering canvas. Overcast inside edges (eye edges) with medium olive green.

5. Work medium olive green and white stitches first on mouth and nose areas of head top before completely filling in areas with light olive green stitches.

6. Stitch remaining pieces. Overcast inside edges on cover top. Overcast feet around toe edges from red dot to red dot, leaving top edges unstitched.

Eyes

1. For each eye, insert shank from front to back through center hole of one eye holder. Place washer over shank up to stitching on back side; glue in place.

2. Center eyes behind openings on head sides. Using light olive green, tack eye holders to stitching on backs of head sides.

Assembly

Note: Throughout all assembly, use light olive green and two stitches per hole as needed to cover edges completely, easing as necessary to fit.

1. Following Fig. 1, Whipstitch cover right side to head right side and one cover end. Whipstitch cover right side to outside tail back and to remaining cover end.

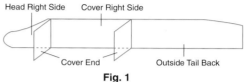

Fig. 1
View shows inner side of assembly

2. Following Fig. 2, Whipstitch cover left side to head left side and cover end. Whipstitch cover left side to inside tail back and to cover end.

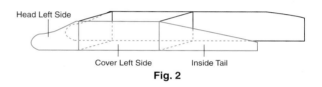

Fig. 2

3. Following Fig. 3, with wrong sides facing, Whipstitch inside tail to outside tail front. Whipstitch tail top to cover end, inside tail and outside tail front.

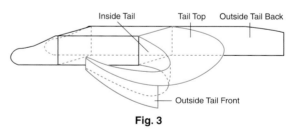

Fig. 3

4. Following Fig. 4, Whipstitch outside tail back to outside tail front and to tail top. Whipstitch tail bottom to tail sides; Whipstitch to cover end.

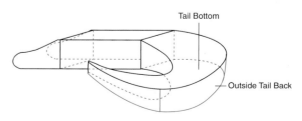

Fig. 4

5. Following Fig. 5, Whipstitch head top to head sides from blue dot to blue dot. Whipstitch head top to head bottom and to cover end. Whipstitch head bottom to head sides and cover end.

6. Whipstitch cover top to cover sides, ends, head top and tail top, working through all layers. Overcast bottom edges of sides, Whipstitching top edges of feet between red dots to corresponding sides between brackets while Overcasting. ■

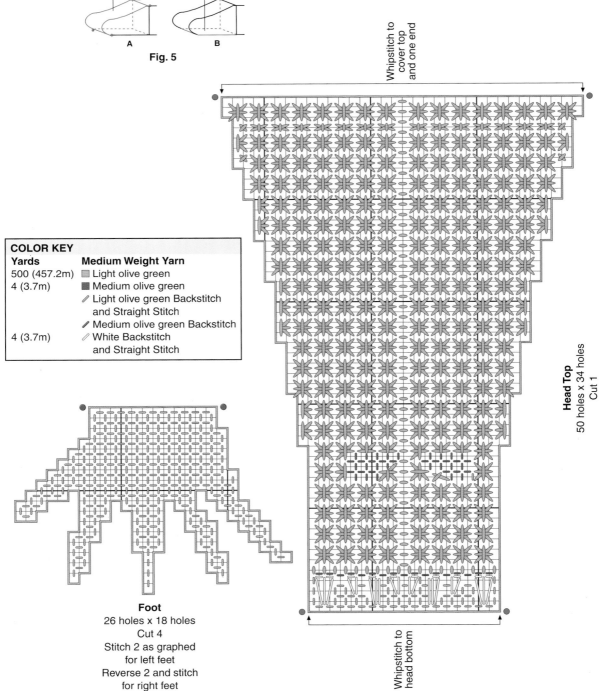

Head Top

Head Bottom

A

B

Fig. 5

COLOR KEY

Yards	Medium Weight Yarn
500 (457.2m)	☐ Light olive green
4 (3.7m)	■ Medium olive green
	✎ Light olive green Backstitch and Straight Stitch
	✎ Medium olive green Backstitch
4 (3.7m)	✎ White Backstitch and Straight Stitch

Whipstitch to cover top and one end

Head Top
50 holes x 34 holes
Cut 1

Whipstitch to head bottom

Foot
26 holes x 18 holes
Cut 4
Stitch 2 as graphed
for left feet
Reverse 2 and stitch
for right feet

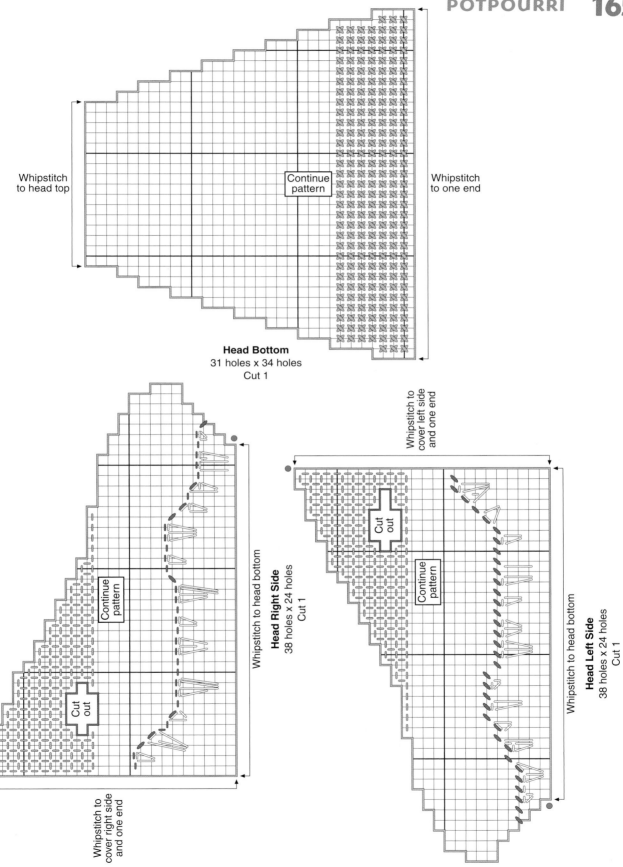

Whipstitch to head top

Continue pattern

Whipstitch to one end

Head Bottom
31 holes x 34 holes
Cut 1

Continue pattern

Cut out

Whipstitch to head bottom

Head Right Side
38 holes x 24 holes
Cut 1

Whipstitch to cover right side and one end

Whipstitch to cover left side and one end

Cut out

Continue pattern

Whipstitch to head bottom

Head Left Side
38 holes x 24 holes
Cut 1

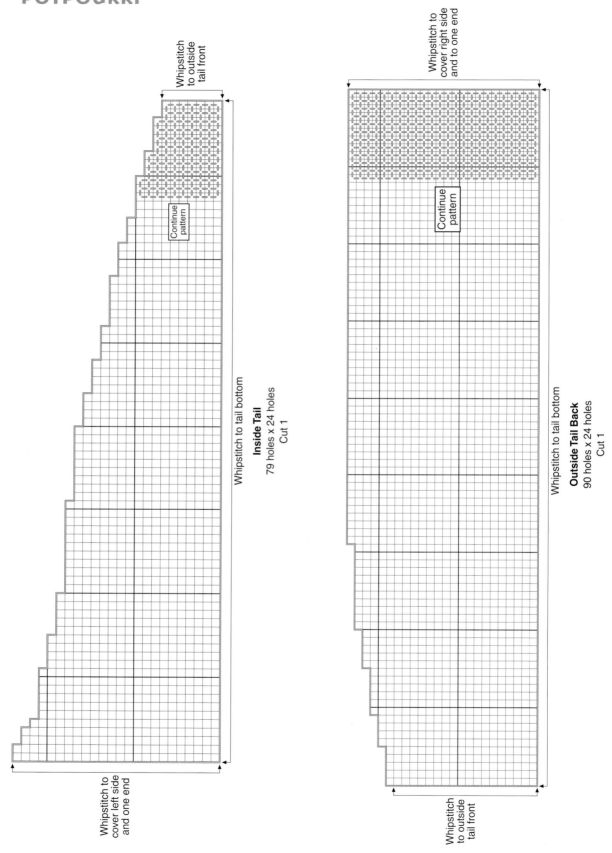

Whipstitch to outside tail front

Continue pattern

Whipstitch to tail bottom
Inside Tail
79 holes x 24 holes
Cut 1

Whipstitch to cover left side and one end

Whipstitch to cover right side and to one end

Continue pattern

Whipstitch to tail bottom
Outside Tail Back
90 holes x 24 holes
Cut 1

Whipstitch to outside tail front

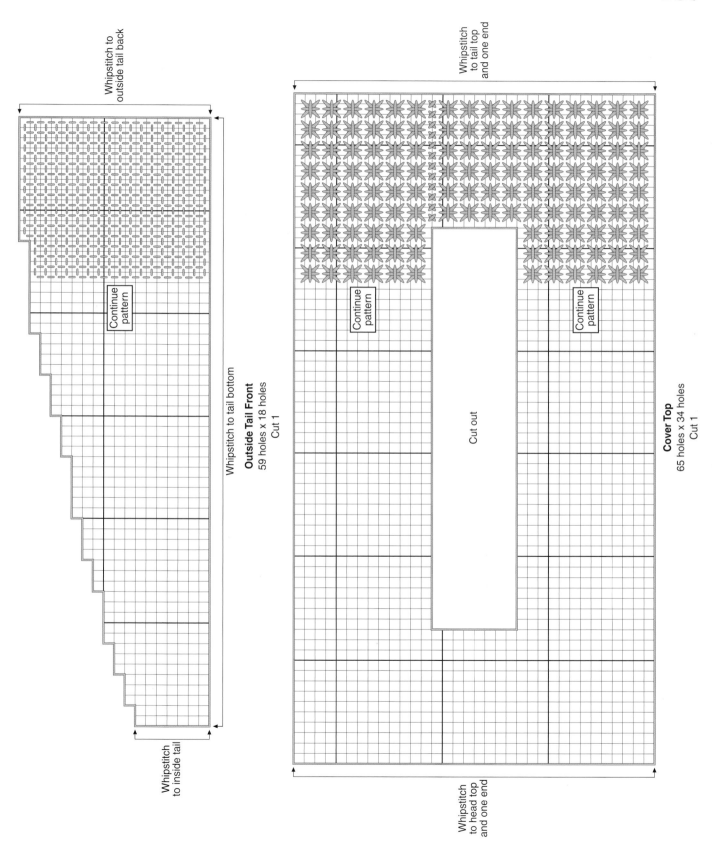

Whipstitch to outside tail back

Whipstitch to tail bottom

Outside Tail Front
59 holes x 18 holes
Cut 1

Continue pattern

Whipstitch to inside tail

Whipstitch to tail top and one end

Continue pattern

Continue pattern

Cut out

Cover Top
65 holes x 34 holes
Cut 1

Whipstitch to head top and one end

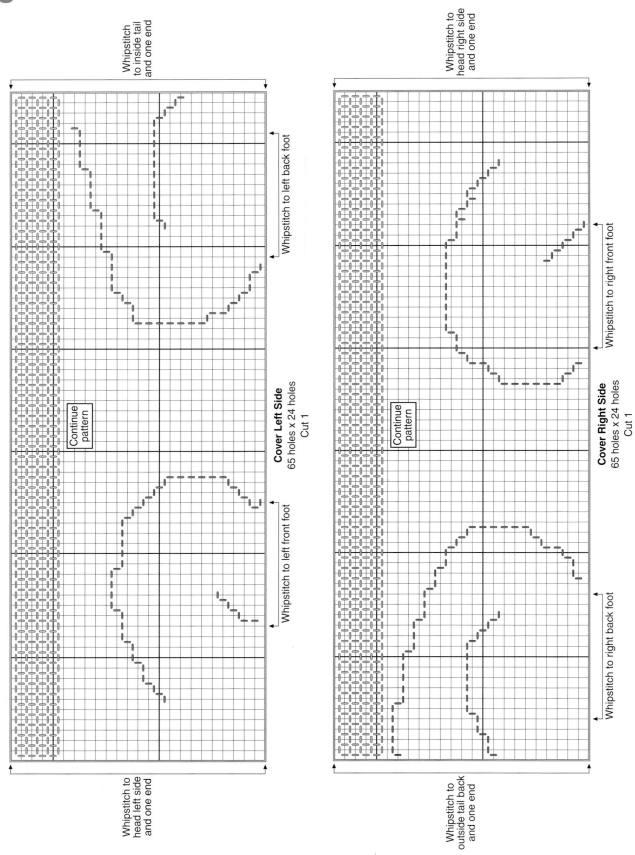

Whipstitch to inside tail and one end

Whipstitch to left back foot

Cover Left Side
65 holes x 24 holes
Cut 1

Continue pattern

Whipstitch to left front foot

Whipstitch to head left side and one end

Whipstitch to head right side and one end

Whipstitch to right front foot

Cover Right Side
65 holes x 24 holes
Cut 1

Continue pattern

Whipstitch to right back foot

Whipstitch to outside tail back and one end

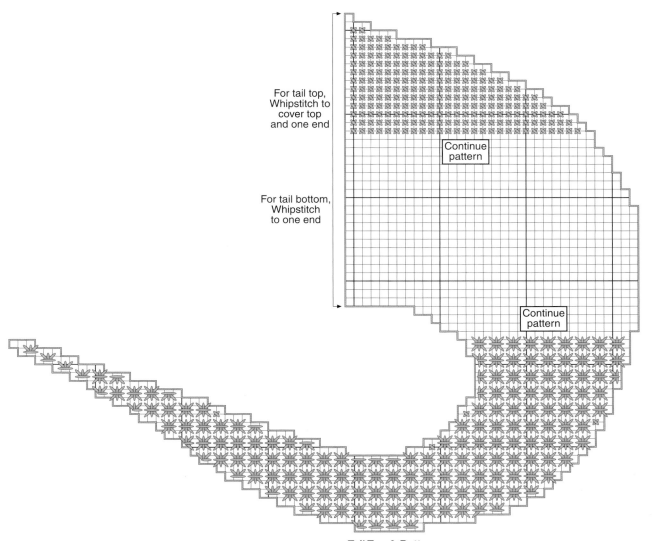

For tail top,
Whipstitch to
cover top
and one end

For tail bottom,
Whipstitch
to one end

Continue
pattern

Continue
pattern

Tail Top & Bottom
73 holes x 62 holes
Cut 2
Stitch tail top following
Smyrna Cross Stitch pattern
Reverse tail bottom
and stitch following
Cross Stitch pattern

COLOR KEY

Yards	Medium Weight Yarn
500 (457.2m)	☐ Light olive green
4 (3.7m)	■ Medium olive green
	⟋ Light olive green Backstitch and Straight Stitch
	⟋ Medium olive green Backstitch
4 (3.7m)	⟋ White Backstitch and Straight Stitch

170 Hot–Pink Purse

Continued from page 152

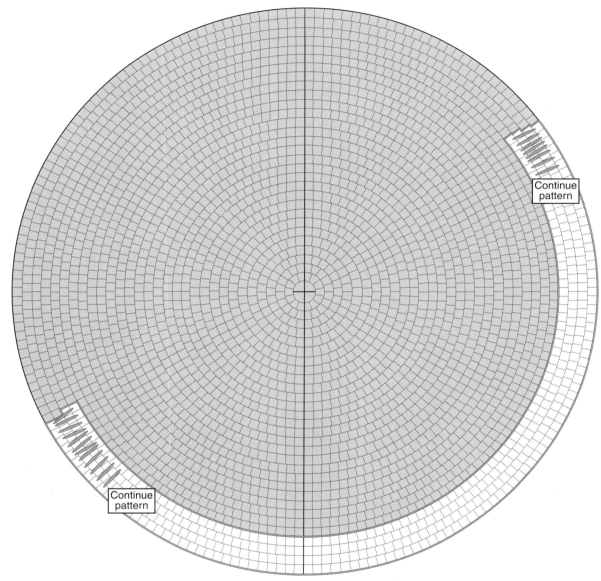

Continue
pattern

Continue
pattern

Handle
Cut 2 from 9-inch radial circles,
cutting away gray area
Reverse 1 before stitching

COLOR KEY	
Yards	**Bulky Weight Eyelash Yarn**
128 (117.1m)	▨ Hot pink #195 (2 strands)
	¹/₈-Inch Ribbon
15 (13.8m)	▢ Silver #001 (2 strands)

Color numbers given are for Lion Brand Fun Fur
Article #320 bulky weight eyelash yarn and
Kreinik ¹/₈-inch Ribbon.

Continued from page 153

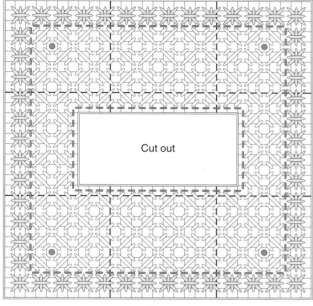

Top
29 holes x 29 holes
Cut 1

Side
29 holes x 37 holes
Cut 4

COLOR KEY		
Yards	**Medium Weight Yarn**	
70 (64m)	☐ Pink	
60 (54.9m)	☐ White	
	6-Strand Embroidery Floss	
10 (9.2m)	✎ Rose Backstitch	
	● Rose French Knot	

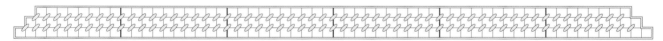

Ribbon
60 holes x 3 holes
Cut 4

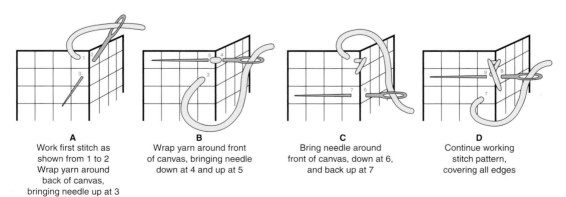

A
Work first stitch as
shown from 1 to 2
Wrap yarn around
back of canvas,
bringing needle up at 3

B
Wrap yarn around front
of canvas, bringing needle
down at 4 and up at 5

C
Bring needle around
front of canvas, down at 6,
and back up at 7

D
Continue working
stitch pattern,
covering all edges

Binding Stitch

Continued from page 155

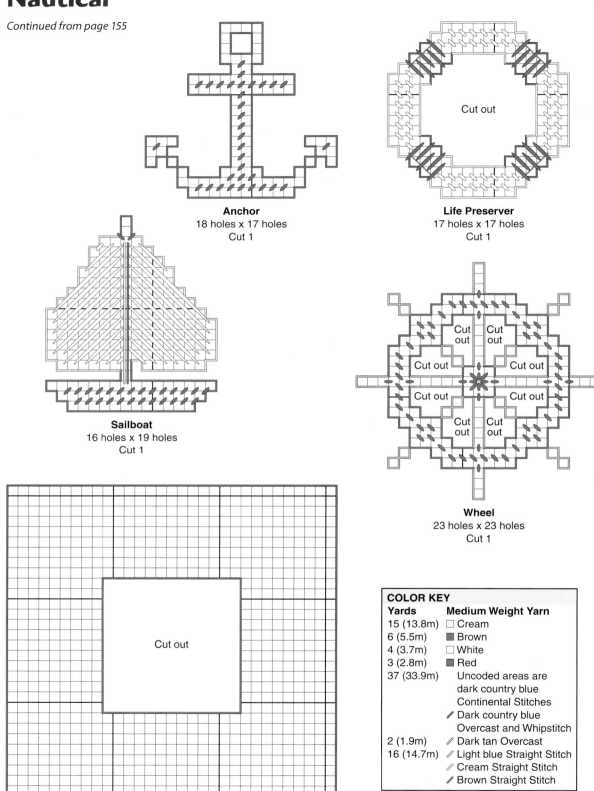

Anchor
18 holes x 17 holes
Cut 1

Life Preserver
17 holes x 17 holes
Cut 1

Sailboat
16 holes x 19 holes
Cut 1

Cut out

Cut out

Cut out

Cut out

Cut out

Cut out

Cut out

Cut out

Wheel
23 holes x 23 holes
Cut 1

Cut out

Top
31 holes x 31 holes
Cut 1

COLOR KEY	
Yards	**Medium Weight Yarn**
15 (13.8m)	☐ Cream
6 (5.5m)	■ Brown
4 (3.7m)	☐ White
3 (2.8m)	■ Red
37 (33.9m)	Uncoded areas are dark country blue Continental Stitches
	✏ Dark country blue Overcast and Whipstitch
2 (1.9m)	✏ Dark tan Overcast
16 (14.7m)	✏ Light blue Straight Stitch
	✏ Cream Straight Stitch
	✏ Brown Straight Stitch

Continued from page 159

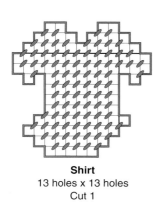

Shirt
13 holes x 13 holes
Cut 1

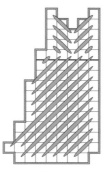

Dress
9 holes x 15 holes
Cut 1

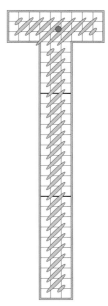

Clothesline Pole
9 holes x 28 holes
Cut 2

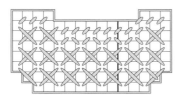

Laundry Basket
15 holes x 8 holes
Cut 1

COLOR KEY

Yards	Medium Weight Yarn
11 (10.1m)	□ White
10 (9.2m)	■ Forest
5 (4.6m)	▨ Tan
3 (2.8m)	■ Red
3 (2.8m)	■ Dark country blue
3 (2.8m)	▨ Bright pink
2 (1.9m)	▨ Salmon
2 (1.9m)	▨ Medium clay
1 (1m)	▨ Lavender
1 (1m)	■ Dark brown
1 (1m)	Magenta
45 (41.2m)	Uncoded areas on white background are light blue Continental Stitches
27 (24.7m)	Uncoded areas on green background are green Continental Stitches
	⁄ Light blue Overcast and Whipstitch
	⁄ Green Overcast and Whipstitch
	⁄ White Backstitch
1 (1m)	⁄ Black Backstitch
2 (1.9m)	Yellow French Knot
	6-Strand Embroidery Floss
1 (1m)	⁄ White Backstitch, Straight Stitch and Running Stitch
	● Attach string

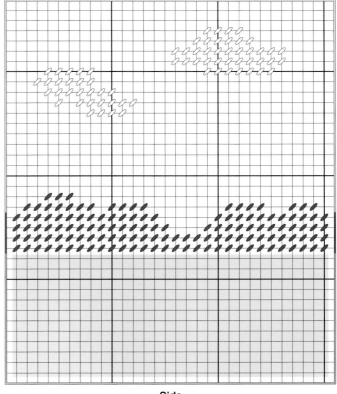

Side
31 holes x 37 holes
Cut 3

Stitch Guide

Use the following diagrams to expand your plastic canvas stitching skills. For each diagram, bring needle up through canvas at the red number one and go back down through the canvas at the red number two. The second stitch is numbered in green. Always bring needle up through the canvas at odd numbers and take it back down through the canvas at the even numbers.

Background Stitches

The following stitches are used for filling in large areas of canvas. The Continental Stitch is the most commonly used stitch. Other stitches, such as the Condensed Mosaic and Scotch Stitch, fill in large areas of canvas more quickly than the Continental Stitch because their stitches cover a larger area of canvas.

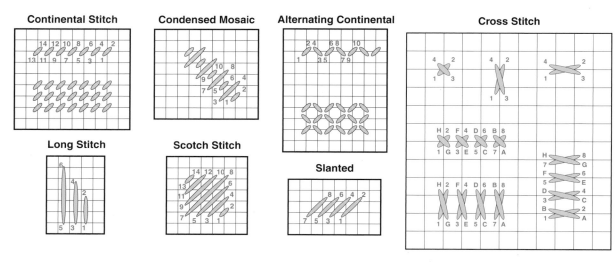

Embroidery Stitches

These stitches are worked on top of a stitched area to add detail to the project. Embroidery stitches are usually worked with one strand of yarn, several strands of pearl cotton or several strands of embroidery floss.

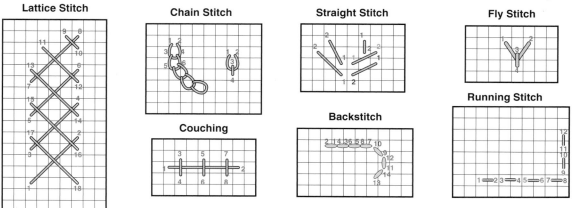

Embroidery Stitches

French Knot

Bring needle up through canvas.

Wrap yarn around needle 1 to 3 times, depending on desired size of knot; take needle back through canvas through same hole.

Lazy Daisy

Bring yarn needle up through canvas, then back down in same hole, leaving a small loop. Then, bring needle up inside loop; take needle back down through canvas on other side of loop.

Loop Stitch/Turkey Loop Stitch

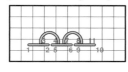

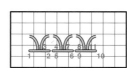

The top diagram shows this stitch left intact. This is an effective stitch for giving a project dimensional hair. The bottom diagram demonstrates the cut loop stitch. Because each stitch is anchored, cutting it will not cause the stitches to come out. A group of cut loop stitches gives a fluffy, soft look and feel to your project.

Specialty Stitches

The following stitches can be worked either on top of a previously stitched area or directly onto the canvas. Like the embroidery stitches, these too add wonderful detail and give your stitching additional interest and texture.

Satin Stitches

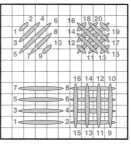

Smyrna Cross

Finishing Stitches

Overcast/Whipstitch

Overcasting and Whipstitching are used to finish the outer edges of the canvas. Overcasting is done to finish one edge at a time. Whipstitching is used to stitch two or more pieces of canvas together along an edge. For both Overcasting and Whipstitching, work one stitch in each hole along straight edges and inside corners, and two or three stitches in outside corners.

Lark's Head Knot

The Lark's Head Knot is used for a fringe edge or for attaching a hanging loop.

Special Thanks

We would like to acknowledge and thank the following designers whose original work has been published in this collection. We appreciate and value their creativity and dedication to designing quality plastic canvas projects!

Debra Arch
Betsy Bear, Dazzling Dahlia, Fresh as a Daisy, Hot-Pink Purse

Angie Arickx
Christmas Cottage, Flowery Bronze, Light & Shadow Roses, Southwest Star & Arrow, Star-Spangled, Sunflower Pinwheel, Vanity Tray

Glenda Chamberlin
Flower Garden, Slice of Watermelon

Mary T. Cosgrove
Pool Shark

D.K. Designs
Autumn Leaves, Neon Bursts, Red, White & Blue, Shadow Diamonds

Nancy Dorman
Flower Shop, Pink Ribbon, Poinsettia, Snowman

Janelle Giese
Desktop Pets, Heart's Delight

Mildred Goeppel
Halloween, Music Lovers

Betty Hansen
Game Time

Patricia Klesh
Butterflies & Bugs

Christina Laws
Kitty

Alida Macor
God Bless You, Rooster, Spring Tulip Garden, Swamp Angels

Terry Ricioli
Starfish, Tropical Fish

Deborah Scheblein
Country Clothesline, Hearts, Nautical, Strawflowers

Laura Victory
Santa

Joanne Wetzel
Alligator

Kathy Wirth
Bow-Tie Kitty, Daisies, Polka-Dot Chicken, Under the Sea

Gina Woods
Elephant, Garden Path, Goose in the Pond, Wildflowers

Buyer's Guide

When looking for a specific material, first check your local craft and retail stores, and the Internet. If you are unable to locate a product, contact the manufacturers listed below for the closest retail source in your area or a mail-order source.

Customer Service
Caron International
P.O. Box 222
Washington, NC 27889
www.caron.com

Coats & Clark
(Red Heart)
(800) 648-1479
www.coatsandclark.com

Darice
Mail-order source:
Schrock's International
P.O. Box 538
Bolivar, OH 44612
(800) 426-4659

DMC Corp.
Mail-order source:
Herrschners Inc.
(800) 441-0830
www.herrschners.com

Kreinik Mfg. Co. Inc.
(800) 537-2166
www.kreinik.com

Lion Brand Yarn Co.
(800) 258-9276
www.lionbrand.com

Uniek
Mail-order source:
Annie's Attic
(800) 282-6643
www.anniesattic.com